MW00810385

IMAGES
of America

MANZANAR

Manzanar War Relocation Center is seen from above, looking north, in this 1944 aerial survey photograph. U.S. Highway 395 is at right; at far right is the Los Angeles Aqueduct. The Manzanar Airport, built in 1940 for military training, is partially obscured for wartime security. Also visible are wide firebreaks between blocks of highly flammable barracks. Internees farmed 500 acres, visible on both sides of the fenced living area. (Courtesy City of Los Angeles Department of Water and Power.)

ON THE COVER: Mount Williamson, at 14,370 feet the second highest peak in the Sierra Nevada, towers over a street of barracks at Manzanar War Relocation Center in 1944. (Courtesy Archie Miyatake, Toyo Miyatake Collection.)

IMAGES
of America

MANZANAR

Jane Wehrey

ARCADIA
PUBLISHING

Copyright © 2008 by Jane Wehrey
ISBN 978-1-5316-3728-6

Published by Arcadia Publishing
Charleston, South Carolina

Library of Congress Catalog Card Number: 2007939182

For all general information contact Arcadia Publishing at:
Telephone 843-853-2070
Fax 843-853-0044
E-mail sales@arcadiapublishing.com
For customer service and orders:
Toll-Free 1-888-313-2665

Visit us on the Internet at www.arcadiapublishing.com

A 2005 view of the southern Owens Valley, looking south, shows Manzanar and part of the former War Relocation Center site. The camp auditorium, built in 1944 and now restored as an interpretive center for Manzanar National Historic Site, is at center. Visible also are portions of the camp road system and 36 residential blocks; concrete slab alignments show the location of latrines and laundry rooms. U.S. Highway 395, through the center of the photograph, is the main road through the valley. (Courtesy Michel Wehrey.)

CONTENTS

ACKNOWLEDGMENTS

All of those who have lived or worked at Manzanar over more than 150 years are the creators of its remarkable history, and my gratitude goes first to them. That history is now under the stewardship of the superb National Park Service staff at Manzanar National Historic Site, led by Supt. Tom Leatherman. All have been supportive of this project, but in particular, I wish to thank Chief of Interpretation Alisa Lynch for her generous assistance in many areas and park rangers Mark Hachtmann and Richard Potashin for help with photograph searches and information. My warm appreciation goes also to Alan Miyatake and his father, Archie, who granted use of and reproduced the Toyo Miyatake images included here. At the Eastern California Museum in Independence, California, Beth Porter and Roberta Harlan were of invaluable help with photograph searches and reproduction. Thank you also to the following: Mauricio Hermosillo and Genie Guerard, UCLA Special Collections; Carolyn Marr, Museum of History and Industry in Seattle; Chris Plakos, Los Angeles Department of Water and Power in Bishop, California; Dace Taube, University of Southern California Libraries; Julie Thomas, California State University Sacramento Library; Barbara Moss, Laws Railroad Museum and Historic Site in Bishop, California; and Jane Nakasako, Japanese American National Museum in Los Angeles.

It was a special pleasure to work with these people, many former Manzanar residents, who gave permission to include images from their collections: Mary Nomura, Isao Sakurai, Fred Causey Jr., Art Williams, Rosie Kakuuchi, Mae Kakehashi, Dolores Pratt, Bruce Embrey, John Bandhauer, Lillian Matsumoto, Peter Kreider, Susan and Martin Powell, Rose Honda, and Joan Beyers. Others who contributed are Greg Murakami, Ann Bell, Catherine Wehrey, Jonathan Fish, and Gena Philibert-Ortega. For his assistance, patience, and enthusiasm, I am grateful to John Poultney, my editor at Arcadia Publishing. And thank you as always to Michel Wehrey.

Concession stands, musical entertainment, and farm exhibits attracted more than 5,000 internees and local residents to the two-day Fall Fair at Manzanar War Relocation Center in September 1943. (Courtesy National Park Service, Manzanar National Historic Site.)

INTRODUCTION

Manzanar, Spanish for "apple orchard," began soon after 1900 in the dream of a fruit-growing empire and today is a national symbol of America's decision at the onset of World War II to confine thousands of its citizens of Japanese ancestry behind barbed wire. But Manzanar's saga reaches back to other earlier dreams and tragedies. It is a story of not simply a single community, but many, whose pasts rest, often uneasily, one atop the other.

Each took root in a landscape of rugged beauty set in the isolated Owens Valley of eastern California. There, streams tumble down from the jagged crest of the Sierra Nevada, and barely 20,000 people live in a land of more than 900 square miles. Native people, called by white explorers the Owens Valley Paiute, subsisted undisturbed for 600 years on the valley's plants and wildlife before the wave of white settlement that swept across the West in the 19th century finally reached them. In the early 1860s, miners, with the gleam of silver in their eyes, crossed the Sierra into the valley, and ranchers followed close behind. When the Paiute fought to keep their land and way of life, the U.S. Army removed hundreds to a distant reservation in Southern California.

Especially attractive to homesteaders was the well-watered area known as George's Creek set against the Sierra Nevada midway between outposts at Independence and Lone Pine. For nearly four decades, ranching and farming occupied the cattlemen and their families who settled there. John Shepherd's 1,300-acre ranch, with its fertile soil and two streams, was among the most prosperous. Southern California developer George Chaffey bought Shepherd's property in 1905, and in 1910, his company subdivided it for a fruit-growing colony called the Manzanar Irrigated Farms. With an innovative, mutually owned irrigation system and 20,000 apples trees brought from Washington, Manzanar grew into a community of 200 over the next 15 years and produced apples, pears, and peaches of exceptional quality. But the presence of the Los Angeles Aqueduct, completed in 1913, cast a long shadow over all agriculture in the Owens Valley, and by 1926, Los Angeles owned all of Manzanar's orchard lands and their prized water rights. Though fruit-growing continued under Los Angeles management, the area gradually declined, and by 1935, the last family was gone.

In the aftermath of Japan's surprise attack on Pearl Harbor on December 7, 1941, Manzanar was transformed from a sleepy abandoned orchard to a mile-square, prison-like camp, one of 10 across the country. Over 10,000 people of Japanese ancestry, two-thirds of them American citizens, were brought there to live, most for the duration of World War II. In that time, they overcame primitive conditions and their own internal divisions, and, together with the War Relocation Authority staff charged with overseeing them, they created a livable wartime city.

Common threads weave through these pasts: groups of uprooted people and a landscape coveted for its water and resources. Their communities, moreover, created specific versions of what they wanted to become and how they wished to be remembered and used photographs to convey those ideals. White pioneers like John Shepherd and his family submitted to tedious early photography to record the island of civility and Euro-American values that his large Victorian home and seven well-attired children represented in the empty Owens Valley wilderness. Photographs of the valley's native people complemented that pioneer story, showing how they benefited from the paternal embrace of those same values. Agricultural subdivisions of the early 20th century, such as George Chaffey's Manzanar Irrigated Farms, relied on colorful advertising, then called booster literature, to promote a vision of prosperity that would entice buyers and produce corporate profits.

As the removal of Japanese Americans unfolded in 1942, the government authorized a corps of photographers to record it. War Relocation Authority (WRA) photographers Clem Albers, Francis Stewart, and Dorothea Lange visited Manzanar in its early weeks, and Lange and Stewart returned in 1943. The WRA did not immediately formulate a photography policy, but military regulations allowed only WRA photographers, and others granted permission, to work in the camps. Their largely unspoken task was to cast the relocation in positive terms and help eliminate any qualms fearful white Americans had about depriving thousands of fellow citizens of their guaranteed rights.

Dorothea Lange was already well-known for her social activism and harrowing images of Depression-era migrant workers, and she used her large body of removal photographs to explore the physical, psychological, and social effects of the government's policy on the incarcerated people. Most of the photographs were never published during the war. Manzanar Project Director Ralph Merritt invited his friend Ansel Adams to photograph the camp as it evolved. During visits in 1943 and 1944, Adams produced more than 200 of his starkly elegant images. Set amid the grandeur of the Owens Valley environment, they portray Manzanar's residents as loyal Americans successfully adapting to life in camp.

A successful photographer in the Little Tokyo section of Los Angeles before his removal to Manzanar, Toyo Miyatake hid a lens and film holder in his luggage, and once in camp asked a carpenter to build a crude camera box from wood scraps. Working early in the morning, he documented Manzanar life for nearly nine months before being noticed. Project director Ralph Merritt concurred with Miyatake's insistence that photographing the camp was his historic duty, and he allowed him to continue, but with a WRA employee called in to release the shutter. Miyatake eventually worked with few restrictions and produced some 1,000 images that document aspects of camp life not otherwise recorded on film.

Few images remain of the camp's aftermath, when buildings were hauled off and sand gradually covered much of what remained of the mile-square city. Local veterans lived for a time in the former staff barracks, but, like the former internees of Manzanar who descended into a long silence about their time in camp, Owens Valley residents, too, wanted to put behind them those four years and the place many called "Jap Camp."

The decades-long effort to gain recognition for Manzanar led to designations as a California State Landmark, a National Historic Landmark, and, in 1992, a National Historic Site. Today a new, nonresident community includes National Park Service staff and nearly 90,000 visitors annually. Among them are many who once lived at Manzanar.

Proprietor R. J. Bandhauer stands in front of his general store at Independence Avenue and Francis Street in Manzanar in this 1922 photograph. (Courtesy John Bandhauer.)

One

A NEIGHBOR'S FIELD

Miners and ranchers crossed the Sierra Nevada into the Owens Valley starting in 1860, and within months, their presence had devastated the way of life of 1,800 native people who had occupied the land for at least 600 years. Called by whites the Owens Valley Paiute, they lived in camps near more than 40 Sierra streams, subsisting on the plants and wildlife of the valley's high desert environment. Named for a friendly Paiute headman, George's Creek was among the largest of the streams, and the area surrounding it was green and well-watered. Settlers claimed homesteads nearby and turned cattle out to graze in the lush grasslands that were the Paiutes' food sources. Desperate as winter approached, the Paiute raided white ranches and stole cattle, and a U.S. Army unit was sent to intervene. Soldiers removed nearly 1,000 of the valley's native people in July 1863 in a forced march 200 miles across the desert to Fort Tejon.

Rancher John Shepherd and his young family had arrived at George's Creek the same year, and in 1864, he claimed a 160-acre homestead 3 miles north, near the creek later named for him. After the earthquake that leveled much of the southern Owens Valley in 1872, he built a nine-room Victorian home that became an Owens Valley landmark and popular stopping place for travelers. The Paiute, meanwhile, had gradually drifted back to the valley, and, with few other options, took up work on the white ranches that had displaced them. Men proved skillful as irrigators, and women worked as laundresses or in the fields winnowing grain. Shepherd employed at least 30 Paiute who lived in a camp west of the ranch house. As was the custom, they took his surname as their own. With their help and labor, Shepherd grew wealthy raising cattle and horses, and by 1900, he owned over 1,300 acres, including most of the future Manzanar War Relocation Center.

Ancestors of the Owens Valley Paiute women, shown here around 1922, lived in villages of willow shelters (below) near the valley's streams. They gathered grasses, plants, and insects from the meadows and hunted rabbits and other small game that populated the valley floor. Each fall, they moved into the Sierra and Inyo Mountains to hunt deer and harvest pine nuts, the staple that would see them through the winter. After the harvest, native people from throughout the valley celebrated with a week of trading, gambling, and dancing at the fandango, or Fall Festival, as it was later called. (Courtesy County of Inyo, Eastern California Museum.)

George's Creek's swift stream, fertile soil, and lush meadows attracted dozens of early homesteaders starting in 1862. Headman of the large Paiute village there, Captain George was respected as a treaty-maker in the escalating conflict between Paiute and Shoshone groups and white settlers. His daughter, Jennie, is shown at the George's Creek Paiute Shoshone camp in the late 1890s. (Courtesy County of Inyo, Eastern California Museum.)

John Kispert built this elegant ranch house in 1873 on the George's Creek land he had homesteaded in 1862. Modeled after the Minnesota girlhood home of his wife, Augusta, it replaced the family's original adobe cabin, damaged in the 1872 Owens Valley earthquake. Like other early ranchers, Kispert operated a side business, hauling freight and ore between Los Angeles and the Cerro Gordo silver mines. (Courtesy County of Inyo, Eastern California Museum.)

With nine rooms and water piped to the kitchen, rancher John Shepherd's two-story Victorian home, shown above in 1880, was "the showplace of the Owens Valley," reported the *Inyo Independent*. A rosewood grand piano graced the parlor, and an ornate fountain greeted visitors in front. Apple, walnut, and poplar trees surrounded the home, and a grape arbor connected it to the property's original adobe cabin, seen below at right. Shepherd and his young family arrived at George's Creek in 1863 after a perilous wagon journey across the Sierra. The adobe cabin he built 3 miles north survived the disastrous 1872 earthquake and was later used as a bunkhouse for teamsters stopping over at the ranch on the long trip through the Owens Valley. (Courtesy County of Inyo, Eastern California Museum.)

John Shepherd and his wife, Margaret (seated left of center), are shown in this 1892 photograph with their seven children and two grandchildren. Early news accounts described the Shepherds' "lavish hospitality and graceful living," and their home was a welcoming stopover for weary travelers through the isolated valley. Lively parties hosted by the four Shepherd daughters brought young people from far and wide. (Courtesy County of Inyo, Eastern California Museum.)

Their traditional way of life devastated by white settlement, the Owens Valley's Paiute and Shoshone people went to work on the same ranches that had displaced them earlier. Seen here, Paiute women sack grain in the Gormans' hay field near Independence. (Courtesy County of Inyo, Eastern California Museum.)

John Shepherd employed 30 or more Paiute men and women, including Johnnie Shepherd (left) and his son Louie. Native American workers typically used the Anglo surname of their employer, often as a sign of respect. Shepherd's concern for his workers' welfare earned him their devotion. At his Masonic funeral in 1906, three hundred Paiute and Shoshone came to honor their friend and "chief." (Courtesy County of Inyo, Eastern California Museum.)

With diverse business interests and some 1,300 acres in ranch holdings, including part of the future Manzanar War Relocation Center, John Shepherd was among Inyo County's wealthiest citizens. These 14-mule wagons, driven by teamster Remi Nadeau, hauled hay that Shepherd sold to miners at Cerro Gordo and other camps. (Courtesy Laws Railroad Museum and Historic Site.)

Shepherd's children, and those of the other two dozen families in the area, attended the George's Creek School, shown here just after 1900. From left to right are Edith, Louie, and Aggie Shepherd, children of Owens Valley Paiute who worked for John Shepherd. (Courtesy County of Inyo, Eastern California Museum.)

Author Mary Austin lived at George's Creek in 1893 for a year. While her husband taught at the school, she immersed herself in the ways of the Paiute women who lived nearby, learning basket weaving and the medicinal uses of plants. Moving later to Independence, she penned the classic *Land of Little Rain* that placed her among the West's foremost literary figures. (Courtesy County of Inyo, Eastern California Museum.)

When the eldest Shepherd son, James Edward, married in 1896, John and Margaret Shepherd presented the couple with a portion of the ranch. The young Shepherds built this home around 1900. Internees at Manzanar War Relocation Center later used its foundations for a storage room next to the camp's judo hall. (Courtesy County of Inyo, Eastern California Museum.)

The wagon trip from Shepherd's ranch to the Inyo County seat at Independence, 6 miles north, took nearly a day. Active in civic affairs, John Shepherd was elected a county supervisor in 1874. The third of Inyo County's four courthouses, shown here, was built in 1887. An earthquake destroyed the first in 1872, and fire gutted the second in 1886. (Courtesy County of Inyo, Eastern California Museum.)

Two

THE APPLE ORCHARD

In 1905, John Shepherd sold his 1,300-acre George's Creek ranch to Charles Chaffey, brother of Southern California irrigation developer George Chaffey, for $25,000. The Chaffeys planned to turn Shepherd's and other properties nearby into an apple-growing subdivision modeled after the irrigated citrus colonies George had launched east of Los Angeles. Doing business as the Owens Valley Improvement Company, the Chaffeys and their investors called their venture the Manzanar Irrigated Farms. A town built in the center would be Manzanar, Spanish for "apple orchard."

In the same period, other powerful men from Los Angeles had their own, far grander designs on the region's land and water that would reshape the future of Manzanar and of the entire Owens Valley. Convinced that the water needed for his city to grow could come from the Owens Valley, Los Angeles water superintendent William Mulholland began plans for a 233-mile aqueduct to carry Owens River water south. At the same time, former Los Angeles mayor Fred Eaton quietly bought up 60 miles of land along the river to gain water rights for Los Angeles. Announcement of the huge project in 1905 sent shock waves through the Owens Valley. Aqueduct construction got under way in 1908, but work on Chaffey's project, mired in disputes with Los Angeles over water rights, started only in 1910. But by 1913, when the aqueduct opened, Manzanar had 20,000 apple trees; a town with a community hall, store, and schoolhouse; and the first buyers for its orchard parcels. Mulholland's engineering feat had little effect on Owens Valley agriculture until the early 1920s, when drought and population growth in Los Angeles sent agents back to the valley for more water. By then, Manzanar's apples were renowned for their quality, but the promised fortunes to be made from them had not materialized. The Owens Valley Improvement Company and other owners were ripe for buyout, and by 1926, Los Angeles owned all of Manzanar. Although it kept orchard operations going, the end of the Manzanar orchard community was not far off.

Fortunes in Apples
In Owens Valley
INYO COUNTY – CALIFORNIA

**OWENS
VALLEY
IMPROVEMENT
COMPANY**

Work on the new Manzanar Irrigated Farms orchard project got under way in 1910, when the Owens Valley Improvement Company (OVI) subdivided the first 1,000 acres and laid out a town in the center called Manzanar—Spanish for "apple orchard." Land agents around the state circulated eye-catching brochures like this one that touted the Owens Valley's scenic beauty, fishing and hunting opportunities, and future in agriculture. Promoters also pointed out the new Southern Pacific rail connection to Los Angeles, which opened lucrative markets for Manzanar's future fruit harvests. The promise of "Fortunes in Apples" attracted buyers slowly; their 10-, 20-, or 40-acre parcels came with one share per acre in the Manzanar Water Corporation and the services of a *zanjero*, or "water distributor." The OVI planted 20,000 apple trees brought from Washington, and Manzanar soon had its own store, blacksmith shop, community hall, and school. (Author's collection.)

To irrigate Manzanar's apple, pear, and peach orchards, the Owens Valley Improvement Company installed an innovative gravity-flow system of steel-lined concrete pipe, shown here being manufactured by contractor Van Lutzow (standing second from right) and his crew near the subdivision. Placed underground, the pipes conveyed water once or twice monthly from nearby Shepherd and Bairs Creeks to the highest corner of each parcel. (Courtesy County of Inyo, Eastern California Museum.)

A prominent engineer and irrigation developer in Australia and California's Imperial Valley, George Chaffey is shown, seated, with family at his home in Whittier, California. He and brother William Benjamin developed successful irrigated agricultural colonies, at Ontario and Etiwanda east of Los Angeles, that became models for the Manzanar venture. (Courtesy Peter Kreider and Susan and Martin Powell.)

Consulting engineers inspect the proposed route of the Owens River–Los Angeles Aqueduct in 1906 with chief engineer William Mulholland (far right) and assistant chief engineer J. B. Lippincott (center). The consultants later reported, "We find the project admirable in conception and outline and full of promise for the continued prosperity of the City of Los Angeles." (Courtesy City of Los Angeles Department of Water and Power.)

Construction of the 233-mile Los Angeles Aqueduct began in 1908 and took five years. Here a section of canal south of Manzanar is prepared for concrete lining. More than 4,000 men and twice that many livestock built the canals, covered conduits, siphons, tunnels, and reservoirs that still carry water by gravity alone across rugged desert and mountain terrain. (Courtesy City of Los Angeles Department of Water and Power.)

Workers test the diversion gates at the intake north of Independence, where Owens River water flows into the aqueduct. On November 4, 1913, more than 30,000 jubilant Angelenos cheered as the first Owens Valley water tumbled down into the city at the aqueduct's cascade-like terminus. "There it is, take it," chief engineer William Mulholland famously said. (Courtesy City of Los Angeles Department of Water and Power.)

In this recent photograph, the aqueduct takes water south from the intake as it has since 1913. After the aqueduct opened, Owens Valley farmers remained cautiously optimistic about the future. With only surplus water going to Los Angeles, land agents promoted the Owens Valley, calling its agriculture "still in its infancy." (Photograph by author.)

The hub of town life at Manzanar for nearly 25 years, the community hall (above) is seen here in 1912. Built by the Owens Valley Improvement Company, it housed a library, offices, and company living quarters. "The Hall" was also the scene of weddings, funerals, Ladies' Aid Society meetings, and Methodist Episcopal Church services. Adults and children alike turned out for the monthly Farm Bureau meetings. At the potluck suppers that followed, they danced the Virginia reel far into the night to live music provided by local talent. Packing crews later used the hall to process tons of apples, peaches, and pears shipped out from Manzanar. Visible behind it is the general store, where owner Ira Hatfield is shown inside (below) with his wife, Mabel, around 1915. (Both courtesy County of Inyo, Eastern California Museum.)

Few of Manzanar's fruit growers were experienced in farming, but they all shared a lingering dream of land ownership in the West. From Southern California, the Midwest, and even England, they came to Manzanar and formed a close-knit community. "Everyone helped each other out," recalled one resident. These residents shown in an apple orchard include W. C. (center) and Nellie (left of center) Lydston. W. C. was originally from Whittier, California. (Author's collection.)

MANZANAR

OWENS RIVER VALLEY

INYO COUNTY CALIFORNIA

ISSUED BY

Manzanar Commercial Club

Manzanar, California

With land sales slower than expected, business-minded citizens formed the Manzanar Commercial Club to "present the advantages of the country to businessmen and farmers, capitalists, and men of achievement." The people of Manzanar "are progressive and enthusiastic," wrote club president and store owner Ira Hatfield in this publicity brochure. (Courtesy County of Inyo, Eastern California Museum.)

Robert J. Bandhauer (above, at right, with family members in 1925) came from Colorado in 1918 and bought the general store from Ira Hatfield. Inside the store (below) were the town's only telephone and the Manzanar Post Office, where Bandhauer's wife, Vivian, was postmistress. Manzanar residents frequently brought eggs and farm produce to the store to trade for dry goods and staples. The family lived next door, on Independence Avenue, the dirt road that today is U.S. Highway 395. (Both author's collection.)

Across the tree-lined road from the general store was a blacksmith shop and later this garage constructed of blocks hewn from local stone. Shown here in the early 1920s, it was owned by the Shelley family and later operated by the Bandhauer family. (Author's collection.)

The Wickiup, seen here around 1924, stood in a field next to the highway across from the community hall and store. Famous around the Owens Valley, it sold ice cream, apple cider, and cold drinks on hot summer days. At other roadside stands, travelers could buy Manzanar's prize-winning Winesap, Spitzenburg, Rome Beauty, Delicious, and Newtown Pippen apples. (Author's collection.)

Children walked or rode horses to the Manzanar School on Francis Street. By the early 1920s, 50 students were attending grades one through eight. Built in 1912 and seen above in 1921, the schoolhouse had "only two rooms and two outside conveniences, plus a shed for the horses," recalled a former student. Manzanar teams played baseball and joined track meets with schools in Lone Pine and Independence, and the school's two teachers usually boarded with families in the community. Below, the children are dressed up for an Easter ice cream treat at school in this April 1919 photograph. (Both author's collection.)

Manzanar's high school–age students rode this school bus to Owens Valley High School in Independence, 6 miles north. Manzanar resident and high school teacher Mabel Wilder drove the big bus, shown here around 1922. Taking her baby along each morning, she picked up students at the town center and at far-flung ranches and farms all the way to George's Creek. "There were sometimes more students from Manzanar than Independence in the high school," recalls one resident. (Author's collection.)

Baseball games, town picnics in the big grove of cottonwood trees, and ice cream socials helped keep the Manzanar community close-knit and neighborly. The Manzanar men's team, seen here in 1922, played teams from Independence, Lone Pine, and other towns in the Owens Valley, where baseball had been a popular pastime since the late 1800s. (Author's collection.)

Limits on fishing and hunting were generous or nonexistent in the Owens Valley of the 1920s, making them the most popular recreational activities for visitors and locals alike. These Manzanar hunters display their bounty in a photograph taken in front of the town's service station and garage around 1922. (Author's collection.)

Children spend a carefree afternoon on this big orchard swing at Manzanar in the mid-1920s. By 1918, the young apple trees planted six years earlier were producing commercial-size quantities of the large, juicy apples Manzanar would be known for. The Manzanar Fruit and Canning Company handled packing, shipping, and selling of the harvests under patent, and while some fruit stayed in the valley for local markets, most was shipped out by rail, north to Nevada or south to Los Angeles. Manzanar apples captured ribbons at the state fair and were soon in demand throughout the state and in the Midwest. Wind and late frosts, however, often kept production low, and the promised fortunes to be made from them didn't materialize. (Courtesy County of Inyo, Eastern California Museum.)

Tensions mounted in the Owens Valley as Los Angeles took control of more land and water rights in the 1920s. Protestors seized the aqueduct on November 24, 1924, at the Alabama Gates spillway south of Manzanar and released the huge flow of water across the desert. Several hundred people, a mariachi band, and dozens of news reporters joined the four-day festivities. (Author's collection.)

When Los Angeles agents began buying up land at Manzanar in 1924, the Owens Valley Improvement Company was one of the first to sell. As Manzanar's sole landowner by 1926, Los Angeles continued orchard operations and that year harvested a record 12 carloads of pears and 37 of apples, with the latter shipped for sale under this City of Los Angeles label. (Courtesy County of Inyo, Eastern California Museum.)

Los Angeles Sunday Times
FARM AND ORCHARD MAGAZINE

SUNDAY MORNING, JUNE 13, 1926.

Los Angeles Makes Hay in Owens Valley

Metropolis of West Acquiring Farms so Fast It Has to Don Overalls to Keep 'Em Up—Has Tenants for Large Acreage and Seeks More—The Ambitious Program

BY HAROLD M. FINLEY

WANTED—Experienced dairymen, hay and grain farmers, deciduous orchardists, small fruit growers, truck gardeners, cattle and hog feeders, poultry raisers and general farmers to take over suitable tracts of land under unusually favorable leases in old established agricultural community. Good soil, ample water, dependable markets. A genuine opportunity for the real farmer with only a limited capital. APPLY CITY OF LOS ANGELES, OWNER.

YES, it's true! The metropolis of the West has added farming to its long list of varied activities. Every property owner and tax-payer in this city of a million and a quarter souls is a stockholder in a great land corporation actively engaged in the [...] tion with the policy being worked out as to the disposition of this acreage, is giving a new aspect to the whole Owens Valley situation. One hears plenty of criticism yet (the writer certainly heard a variety of comment around Bishop two weeks ago,) but there is undeniably less talk now than [...] high up on Rock Creek, a lumbering crew is clearing away timber from what would very conveniently serve as a basin for a much larger body of water, while men employed by the city are widening the road leading to the lake from the Inyo-Mono counties highway. This is mentioned because it is [...] elimination of waste in actual water utilization is to come later, the city's representatives say. In Owens Valley, as about everywhere else in the reclaimed desert areas of California, water is undoubtedly wasted in various ways. The Bishop area in particular is cited as being waterlogged in spots from excessive and ill-timed irrigation. Those farming city lands, it is declared, will have to be more careful in using water. Modern distribution systems are also expected to figure importantly in water saving when Los Angeles really settles down to the farm landlord business and starts making improvements on a wholesale scale.

As seen here, Los Angeles residents avidly followed accounts of their city's Owens Valley agricultural enterprise. Originally intended for groundwater storage management and to help repair the city's image in the valley, the Manzanar orchards and farms nonetheless produced profits for the city of over $14,000 in 1926. (Courtesy County of Inyo, Eastern California Museum.)

Fruit packers have fun on the back stairs of the community hall. Local residents earned extra money picking Manzanar's apples, pears, and peaches. Crews brought in by Consolidated Produce, the shipping company hired by Los Angeles, packed them in the big hall. Late-spring frosts destroyed much of the 1927 crop; "Los Angeles Finds Farming a Hard Game," a *Los Angeles Times* headline read that year. (Courtesy County of Inyo, Eastern California Museum.)

This 1931 aerial survey photograph looking north from Manzanar shows some orchards still in production, with most other agricultural land already reverted to dry fields. Los Angeles shut off irrigation entirely at Manzanar in 1934. The relocation center would later occupy the central portion of this photograph. (Courtesy Air Photo Archive, UCLA Department of Geography.)

The general store and garage, seen here in 1929, stayed in business until 1930. As more people left Manzanar, the City of Los Angeles rented the former farm homes to its own valley employees. The post office closed on December 31, 1929, and the last resident, poultry farmer Clarence Butterfield, was asked by the city to leave in 1935. (Courtesy John Bandhauer.)

Three

EXCLUSION ORDERS

Manzanar's orchards fell into neglect after 1934, but many kept producing, and each fall, local residents harvested their fruit for pies and preserves. Cattle grazed contentedly in the former hay fields, and teenagers raced their jalopies after dark in the deserted orchard rows. Japan's surprise attack on Pearl Harbor on December 7, 1941, shattered that calm in the Owens Valley and across America. War hysteria soon enveloped Pacific coastal cities, but in the Owens Valley, isolated from the coast by the Sierra Nevada, few residents felt in danger. As calls for the removal of all ethnic Japanese from coastal areas grew louder, Pres. Franklin Roosevelt signed Executive Order 9066 on February 19, 1942. Eight days later, military officials appeared in the Owens Valley and selected the orchards and former town site at Manzanar as the location of the first "processing center" for "evacuated" Japanese. Manzanar's isolation, agricultural potential, and access to water and power sources met the military's requirements. But its landowner, Los Angeles, vehemently protested locating the camp within 1 mile of its aqueduct, which was considered a defense installation. Assured of military protection, Los Angeles agreed to a lease of 6,000 acres for the camp.

U.S. Department of Justice officials, meanwhile, had rounded up hundreds of Japanese aliens with ties to Japanese cultural or political activities. Families left behind faced growing isolation and uncertainty about their own futures. Despite the reluctance of many in the military and government to undertake a project clearly in violation of citizen rights, plans for the "gradual and orderly removal" of more than 100,000 ethnic Japanese from Military Area No. 1, along the coast, went forward. Most were taken first to one of 16 assembly centers, usually in converted racetracks and fairgrounds. There they remained, some for up to six months, until the relocation centers were built. The Owens Valley Reception Center at Manzanar, however, was the first and only destination for most of the 10,000 people sent there.

Images like this one, of fireboats attempting to save the USS *West Virginia*, brought home to Americans the grim reality of Japan's attack on Pearl Harbor on December 7, 1941. By early 1942, sightings of Japanese submarines off the Pacific coast had raised fears of an attack on the mainland and fueled a mounting anti-Japanese hysteria. (Department of Defense photograph, courtesy Library of Congress.)

Rumors of sabotage and spying by West Coast residents of Japanese ancestry turned many white Californians against their Japanese neighbors. Reflected in this headline are the war hysteria and decades of racist attitudes that led to Executive Order 9066 and the removal of the region's entire ethnic Japanese population. (Courtesy Library of Congress Prints and Photographs Division, LC-USZ62-17121.)

INYO INDEPENDENT

EXTRA

Established 1870 ◆ *Independence, Calif.*

VOL. LXXI. NO. 37   INDEPENDENCE, INYO COUNTY, CALIFORNIA, FRIDAY, MAR. 6, 1942 $2.50 A YEAR

Jap Resettlement Camp for Valley

Manzanar Site of Japanese Reception Center; Expect 5 to 10 Thousand

Let's Look At This New Development With A Long Range View; An Editorial Of Interest To Every Citizen

With today's announcement of the United States Army action in placing a Japanese "reception center" in the Owens Valley, an unusual story of war-time emergency and protection of vital defense areas along the coast of California is unfolded.

Coming as a complete surprise last Friday was the visit of United States Army Engineers, representatives of Attorney General Biddle and other federal departments. At that time a few citizens of Inyo county were called in at the request of the department of justice to discuss the matter.

These citizens were told that this is a war emergency, that the army had decided on locating a Japanese "reception center" here and that the city had been requested to provide needed

ever, has offered domicile for a part of the population, seeing the possibility of using them in certain agricultural developments in his state.

Now Inyo county comes forward, its people provided with an opportunity to permit a part of our land and natural resources to be used for defense production, possibly of foodstuffs and other needs.

Therefore, isn't it our willing duty to cooperate with the federal government?

The group of seven Inyo citizens thought so, and proceeded to prepare a constructive program in which evacuees could be

General DeWitt to Order Camp Location Here; 8,000 Acres Set Aside for Huge Project

Through an army order expected to be issued momentarily by General DeWitt, some 8000 acres in Owens Valley between Independence and Lone Pine are to be taken over by the army for what is termed as a "reception center" for Japanese to be evacuated from coastal areas, last minute news from Los Angeles to this paper reveals. During the last few days, since the army made plain the Owens Valley site was under serious consideration, there has been nearly continuous conferences between the Federal officials and officials of the City of Los Angeles, who are owners of the land.

Federal officials went to the Owens Valley and selected what one described as "a frowzy dilapidated orchard" called Manzanar as the location of a "reception center" for Japanese Americans. News of the project stunned local residents. To calm fears, this special edition of the *Inyo Independent* appealed to residents' patriotism, calling the camp their contribution to the war effort. (Courtesy the *Inyo Register*.)

Army engineers quickly drew up plans for the Manzanar center. They called for modified Theater of Operations barracks built to the "minimum requirements of health and sanitation." Trucks hauled in more than 6 million board feet of lumber. By March 17, over 1,000 workers hired by Griffith and Company of Los Angeles were putting up barracks at the rate of two per hour. (War Relocation Authority photograph, courtesy National Archives, NWDNS-210-G-B139.)

Assurances of a military police presence helped calm fears of residents in nearby Lone Pine and Independence; a contingent arrived within two days of the start of construction. (Courtesy the Manzanar Committee, Manzanar National Historic Site.)

Truckloads of food, supplies, and equipment arrived daily as the Owens Valley Reception Center went up. Construction workers slept in tents and ate at outdoor kitchens. The first internees to arrive found open sewer trenches and windowless buildings. (Acme Photo, author's collection.)

Construction was barely under way when 81 "voluntary" internees arrived to help set up kitchens, medical care, and other functions. A second contingent of 500 left Southern California's Rose Bowl on March 23 in a 6-mile-long caravan of military trucks and 200 or so private vehicles. Packed with tools, plant seedlings, and household goods, they are seen here turning into Manzanar. (Gift of Jack and Peggy Iwata, Japanese American National Museum, 93.102.190.)

Exclusion orders like this one, posted in downtown San Francisco, gave residents one week to register at a Civil Control Station and be ready for removal. The Wartime Civilian Control Administration posted orders in sequence for the 98 zones within Military Area No. 1. The same army units managed the entire removal. (Courtesy Library of Congress Prints and Photographs Division, LC-USZ62-34565.)

Tagged with his family's identification number, an Issei, or immigrant generation, grandfather awaits removal to an assembly center near Sacramento, California. He was later transferred to one of 10 relocation centers across the country. Most Issei had lived in the United States 30 years or more, but they were barred from citizenship or owning land by anti-Japanese laws enacted in the early 1900s. (War Relocation Authority photograph by Dorothea Lange, courtesy National Archives, NWDNS-210-G-C219.)

Japanese Americans facing removal had a few weeks at most to arrange for businesses and homes. Many entrusted property and belongings to Caucasian friends and neighbors; others were at the mercy of unscrupulous real estate agents. Here wooden planks cover the windows of Higo's Ten Cent Store and other Japanese shops in downtown Seattle. (*Seattle Post-Intelligencer* Collection, courtesy Seattle Museum of History and Industry.)

Military officials removed 227 Japanese and Japanese Americans living on Bainbridge Island, Washington, on March 26, 1942, under Civilian Exclusion Order No. 1. They are shown crossing the Eagledale Dock to board the ferry for Seattle and the train south. Located west of Seattle, near the strategic Bremerton Naval Base, Bainbridge Island was a community of truck farmers and summer homeowners. Successful in strawberry farming, the small Japanese minority had earned the respect of fellow residents. Their swift removal, before an assembly center at nearby Puyallup was ready, was a test of the evacuation process that was marked by confusion and poor communication. After a four-day train journey, they arrived at Manzanar to blowing sand and primitive, partially finished facilities. Assigned as a community to Block 3, they stayed at Manzanar until February 1943, when most transferred at their own request to the Minidoka, Idaho, camp to join other Northwest-area internees. (*Seattle Post-Intelligencer* Collection, courtesy Seattle Museum of History and Industry.)

Families wait at the old Santa Fe Station in Los Angeles, where a special train will take them to the Owens Valley. In advance of posted orders, extended families often moved into one home to be removed together. Military instructions stated that bedding, toilet articles, clothing, eating utensils, and personal effects for each family member were to be packed in suitcases or bundles limited "to that which can be carried by the individual or family group." Crated tools, furniture, and other items could be stored and shipped to Manzanar later. Told they were going to a pioneer community, internees took work clothes, heavy boots, and canned food—like a "compulsory campout," wrote one. (Both photographs by Lee Russell, U.S. Office of War Information Collection, courtesy Library of Congress Prints and Photographs Division.)

Japanese Americans traveling by train arrived at Lone Pine Station, 8 miles south of Manzanar, (above). These internees coming from Elk Grove, California, board buses for the final leg of their removal (below). By mid-April 1942, up to 1,000 people were streaming into the center daily; one month later, the population stood at 7,000. Residents of the last exclusion zone in Military Area No. 1, a community near Sacramento, California, were removed on June 6, two days after the United States' decisive naval victory against the Japanese at Midway Island. (Both photographs by Francis Stewart, War Relocation Authority, courtesy National Archives; above, NWDNS-210-G-520; below, NWDNS-210-G-524.)

Internees' first sight of Manzanar was often obscured by windblown sand from the newly bulldozed landscape. Dust and sand pervaded camp life for months, sifting into clothing and food and leaving sleeping figures outlined on beds each morning. Residents collected tin can lids to nail over knotholes and cracks in walls, ceilings, and floors until wallboard became available. (War Relocation Authority photograph, courtesy National Archives, NWDNS-210-G-B105.)

"The cruel transition of living habits and lifestyle from a civilized society to this degrading situation was hard to understand," wrote internee Shiro Nomura. His family of six occupied a 20-by-25-foot "apartment" with an oil stove, eight cots, and a single lightbulb. Before mattresses became available, residents were issued ticking to fill with straw. (*Los Angeles Examiner* Collection, courtesy University of Southern California Special Libraries and Archival Collections.)

Four

COMMUNITIES
IN CONFINEMENT

Thirty-six drab and depressingly identical barracks blocks, each with 300 or more occupants, functioned as both living and administrative units at Manzanar. Gradually their sameness gave way to unique identities, many formed by internees' prewar ties. Manzanar's 10,000 people came from dozens of communities in Southern California and elsewhere. As the exclusion orders emptied neighborhoods and towns, authorities generally moved their residents to the same camp and often assigned them housing together. At Manzanar, West Los Angeles residents lived in Block 22, while those from the San Fernando Valley occupied Block 28. Bainbridge Island, Washington, strawberry farmers in Block 3 were next to Terminal Island, California, fishermen in Blocks 9 and 10.

Special groups had their own living areas. Children of even partial Japanese heritage without parents or families—those in orphanages and foster care included—came under the mandatory evacuation order. All were brought to Manzanar, and a total of 101 children, together with staff, lived in the landscaped three-building Children's Village set in a firebreak near the pear orchard. Nearby, doctors and nurses had quarters at the hospital; other internee medical workers lived in Blocks 29 and 34 across the street. Often shunned by older Issei fearful of disease, medical personnel formed their own close-knit community. War Relocation Authority staff, including teachers, lived first in Block 7, enduring primitive barracks conditions with internees. By early 1943, the "Beverly Hills of Manzanar," as the WRA area was known to internees, was ready. The 22 well-built, gleaming white barracks were configured as dormitories or family apartments with kitchens and baths and housed nearly 300 staff and their families. Employees had their own mess hall, recreation club, and Victory Garden. Some, including children, socialized with their Nisei (or American-born, second-generation Japanese) counterparts at internee parties, baseball games, and weddings. But others clearly felt the invisible barrier that lay between them. At Project Director Ralph Merritt's insistence, the staff housing was inside the fenced internee living area, a symbolic gesture that, as he later wrote, "we are all in this together."

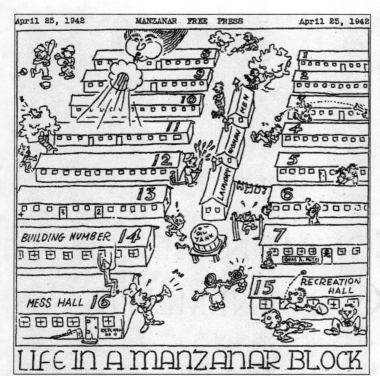

April 25, 1942   MANZANAR FREE PRESS   April 25, 1942

LIFE IN A MANZANAR BLOCK

The internee-produced *Manzanar Free Press* published this graphic soon after the camp opened. Thirty-six blocks, each with 14 residential barracks, became centers of a communal life with little privacy and few comforts. Women especially found the latrines and showers without partitions humiliating. (Courtesy National Park Service, Manzanar National Historic Site.)

Barracks addresses reinforced the camp's stark uniformity, as seen in the upper right of this photograph. (War Relocation Authority photograph by Dorothea Lange, courtesy National Archives, NWDNS-210-G-C873.)

44

Internee photographer Toyo Miyatake and his wife gather in their children's bedroom for this 1943 Ansel Adams photograph. By then, barracks had interior wallboard and linoleum floors, available in a selection of colors. Internee furniture makers produced pieces like those shown, and women made curtains, bedding, and clothing from fabric sold at the camp's general store. (Courtesy Library of Congress Prints and Photographs Division, LC-A351-3-M-36.)

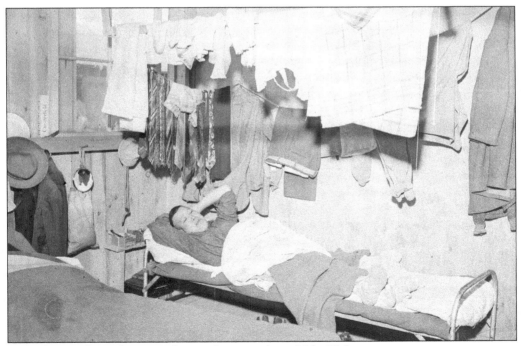

In the first weeks, with up to eight people assigned to a 20-by-25-foot apartment, space was scarce, and furniture promised by camp administration was slow to come. This man hangs shirts and ties in a makeshift closet arrangement. Residents salvaged wood from barracks construction and built rough shelves, cabinets, tables, and chairs. (War Relocation Authority photograph, courtesy National Archives, NWDNS-210-G-B112.)

Women, usually with small children in tow, were often busy in their block laundry rooms, as depicted in this drawing by Estelle Ishigo. A Caucasian artist, she was married to Arthur Ishigo, a Nisei, and accompanied him to Heart Mountain Relocation Center in Wyoming. Laundry and ironing rooms, with cement floors, were favorite places for small boys playing marbles. (Untitled, 1943, Estelle Ishigo, courtesy Japanese American National Museum, 94.195.13.)

The sound of a gong announced three meals a day at each of the camp's 34 mess halls. Supplied by the army quartermaster, food at first was unappealing, especially to many Issei accustomed to Japanese-style foods. Meals improved as more rice became available and better-trained chefs used vegetables, fruit, meat, tofu, and shoyu produced in camp. (War Relocation Authority photograph by Dorothea Lange, courtesy National Archives, NWDNS-210-G-C890.)

46

Long mealtime lines were a fixture of block life (above). To ease the wait in Block 22, kitchen worker Harry Ueno and nurseryman Akira Nishi created the first of several ornamental gardens that internees built next to mess halls. This one in Block 12 (below) was among the most beautiful. With waterfalls, bridges, and landscaping that combined traditional Japanese and American garden styles, the gardens became showcases for the talents of Manzanar's several hundred landscape designers, gardeners, and nurserymen. (Above, War Relocation Authority photograph by Dorothea Lange, courtesy National Archives, NWDNS-210-G-C671; below, War Relocation Authority Collection, UCLA Special Collections.)

Residents of Block 12 gather on August 12, 1943, for this photograph at their mess hall. Its pond and waterfall garden is at right. Internees brought in colorful rocks from the Inyo Mountains and granite boulders from the Sierra Nevada that added texture and symbolism to the garden designs. Block residents took pride in their gardens, together with lawns, rock-lined walkways,

William Katsuki, former landscaper to wealthy Los Angeles residents, created Manzanar's first ornamental barracks garden at his Block 24 home between Buildings 5 and 6. It featured four small ponds with miniature bridges and three large Joshua trees. (War Relocation Authority photograph by Dorothea Lange, courtesy National Archives, NWDNS-210-G-C865.)

flower beds, and other improvements they made. In the "best garden" reader survey sponsored by the *Manzanar Free Press*, gardens in Block 34 and 22 won top honors. Visible at far left is the block's heating-oil tank. (Courtesy National Park Service, Manzanar National Historic Site.)

By August 1942, internees had planted hundreds of flower and vegetable gardens near their barracks and more than 400,000 square feet of lawn. Fences made of tree branches were common at Manzanar because of wartime shortages of wood. (War Relocation Authority photography by Dorothea Lange, courtesy National Archives, NWDNS-21-G-C872.)

The only orphanage in the 10 relocation centers, the Children's Village was home to a total of 101 children. These preschool children have their picture taken on the village's broad lawn. Located in a firebreak apart from the noise and crowding of the blocks, the three well-constructed buildings had dormitories for boys and girls, bathrooms, kitchen, and staff quarters. (Courtesy Lillian Matsumoto.)

Children of all ages lived at the village, and teenage residents were counselors to the younger children. School-age children attended the camp schools and joined camp activities. Older Japanese often looked down on the children of mixed ancestry, or *hapa*, who lived in the village. (War Relocation Authority photograph by Dorothea Lange, courtesy National Archives, NWDNS-210-G-C905.)

In this 1944 group photograph on the lawn, Supt. Harry Matsumoto and his wife, Asst. Supt. Lillian Matsumoto, are at center, surrounded by the children and Children's Village staff. About half of the wartime family they nurtured were true orphans. Parents or families of others were unable to care for them during the internment, and some were the infants of unmarried mothers in the camps. (Courtesy Archie Miyatake, Toyo Miyatake Collection.)

"Games for exercise and out-of-door play, with much sunshine, tended to keep the children healthy and happy," wrote Eva Robbins, superintendent during the last year before the village closed. Preschoolers play on equipment built for them by carpenters in the camp's wood shop. (Author's collection.)

The block manager for each of Manzanar's 34 residential blocks represented residents to camp administration and carried WRA policy information back to them. Early managers included, from left to right, (first row) Karl Yoneda and H. Inouye; (second row) Bill Kito, Ted Akahoshi, Tom Yamazaki, and Harry Nakemura. For many Issei long denied citizenship, electing a block manager was their first voting experience. (War Relocation Authority photograph, National Archives, NWDNS-210-G-D569.)

Managers and administrators discussed internee complaints and camp operations at weekly block managers' assemblies in the town hall. Here *Manzanar Free Press* editor Roy Takeno speaks to the group. Also shown is Lucy Adams, assistant project director for community activities. Managers also supervised maintenance on their blocks, handled emergencies, and distributed soap and lightbulbs. (Ansel Adams photograph, courtesy Library of Congress Prints and Photographs Division, 10479-4, no. 21.)

Businessman and Owens Valley civic leader Ralph Merritt (above, second from left) took over as Project Director in November 1942 despite his stated "strong reservations" about the internment's legality. Confronted with mounting tensions among internees and the effects of months of administrative indecision, he soon earned the internees' respect as an able and compassionate administrator. With him are, from left to right, reports officer Robert Brown, unidentified, War Relocation Authority Director Dillon Meyer, and Assistant Project Director Ned Campbell. The WRA employed an average of 150 personnel, and many worked in the administration building on First Street (below). Internee office workers filled out the staffs of the various departments, and internee gardeners maintained the manicured landscaping in the staff area. (Above, courtesy Archie Miyatake, Toyo Miyatake Collection; below, courtesy National Archives and Manzanar National Historic Site.)

WRA civil engineer Fred Causey Sr. brought his family to Manzanar in 1943. His wife, Mildred, and daughter Ann are seen here at the administration area's distinctive traffic circle. Called by internees the "Beverly Hills" of Manzanar, the 22 WRA buildings housed nearly 300 staff and family. The Causeys lived in a two-bedroom apartment with a kitchen and bath but ate most meals in a staff mess hall. (Courtesy Frederick Causey Jr.)

Some of Manzanar's 35 appointed elementary school teachers gather near the staff apartments for this picture. As sponsors of school clubs and youth groups, they helped improve relations between internees and administration and often gave up wartime ration points to supplement refreshments for class parties. They also supervised Manzanar's internee student teachers. (Merritt Collection, courtesy County of Inyo, Eastern California Museum.)

Daughters of War Relocation Authority employees (above) are seen in front of a staff apartment. Most of the school-age WRA children went to school in Independence, 6 miles north. Some found the isolation of the Owens Valley and life in what many later called the "camp within a camp" hard to take. But "we were a very close-knit group of children and adults," recalls one WRA offspring. The WRA organized an Appointed Personnel Recreation Club and set aside room for a clubhouse. The first issue of the "Manzanar Magpie," a mimeographed staff newspaper, appeared in 1944. Staff and their families showed passes (below) to military police when they left camp and returned. Swimming, hunting, and Saturday night movies in Lone Pine were favorite pastimes outside camp. (Above, courtesy Frederick Causey Jr.; below, courtesy Joan Beyers.)

MANZANAR RELOCATION AREA
CIVILIAN PASS

No. __86__

Good only for __MAR__ __1944__

Name __Joan Davalle__

Position __Daughter of Teacher__

Height __5'1"__ Eyes __Brown__ Hair __Brown__

Robert Th Brown
Asst. Project Director

Signature of Holder

The 99 military police sent to Manzanar to guard the perimeter and control entry had been "trained to kill Japs, not protect them," said their commanding officer, Lt. Harvey Severson. Many were bored by guard duty, and internees resented their armed presence. Some local residents complained of their behavior off-duty, labeling them "misfits." Quartered south of the fenced camp area, they lived first in a tent compound (above) and later in permanent barracks. Shown below is their view from one of eight guard towers completed by November 1942 that reduced the need for foot patrols. Soldiers' attempts to make friends with internees, especially girls, ended when they were ordered by their commander "not to talk to their charges." (War Relocation Authority photographs, National Archives; above photograph by Clem Albers, NWDNS-210-G-B110; below, photograph by Dorothea Lange, NWDNS-210-G-C879.)

Five

A CITY SERVING
A WARTIME PURPOSE

The "wartime purpose" that Project Director Ralph Merritt described for Manzanar was never entirely clear to most of its residents. But it was a city, nonetheless, that began as an instant boomtown of 10,000 people who required food, water, electricity, medical care, and employment. When the first internees arrived, only the barest outline of an infrastructure was in place. Open ditches carried wastewater and sewage, internee cooks heated water in garbage cans on outside stoves, and medical care consisted of one doctor working in a barracks room without running water. Within a few weeks, Manzanar was more habitable, thanks to the efforts of both internees and Caucasian staff. By early 1943, Project Director Ralph Merritt had brought stability to the War Relocation Authority staff and more efficiency to its organization. WRA personnel and internees worked together in nearly every department, with internees often in supervisory positions.

The government's goal of making Manzanar and the other camps as self-sufficient as possible opened hundreds of jobs to internees in farming, medical care, public works, and manufacturing. The 34 mess halls employed 1,500 internees, and others worked in stores, barbershops, and other services. Employment was not mandatory, but 80 percent of eligible internees did have jobs, in part to ease the tedium of daily life in camp. Less of an incentive was the wage scale. A constant source of friction between internees and administration, it was set well below prevailing wage scales on the outside. Unskilled and semiskilled laborers earned $12 a month, skilled workers got $16, and professionals or supervisors received $19. Many jobs included on-the-job training. Internee police and firemen, together with utility workers, social workers, hairdressers, teachers, and cooks, received training that would help fulfill the government's goal of preparing Manzanar's residents to disperse across America.

The barbed-wire fence and eight guard towers surrounding Manzanar gave stark evidence that this was no ordinary American city, despite the nearly 7,000 American citizens who lived there. Lone Pine contractor Charles Summers began work on the first four towers in June 1942 over the objections of some in the War Relocation Authority, who argued that "our direction of effort should be away from surveillance of these people as enemies." The *Manzanar Free Press* reported, "Have you noticed those towers going up around this center and wondered whether those incipient skyscrapers were the prelude to a carnival or a fair?" By November, all eight towers were in use. Their powerful searchlights remained on all night at Project Director Ralph Merritt's order, "for the comfort of mind of local residents." With a reduced military police presence by the summer of 1943, they were not manned full-time, and by December, they had been abandoned. Photographs of the towers and barbed-wire fence are few, as military regulations prohibited WRA photographers from including them in their images. (Courtesy Archie Miyatake, Toyo Miyatake Collection.)

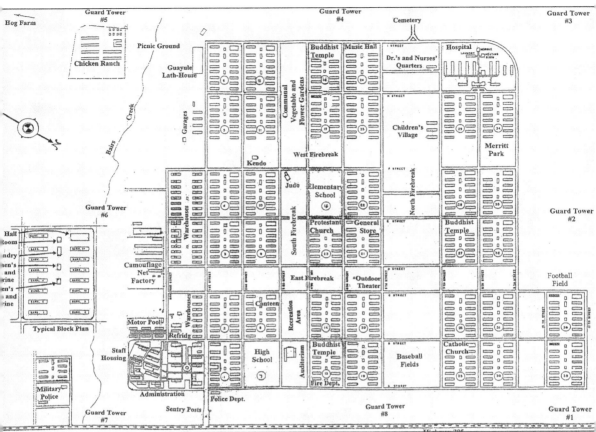

This War Relocation Authority site plan of Manzanar from 1946 shows the layout of the 36 blocks and the firebreaks, together with features added during the nearly four years of camp operation. The WRA staff housing area was within the fenced camp area, at lower left of center. The military police compound, "Camp Manzanar," is outside the fence at lower left. U.S. Highway 395, shown at the lower edge of map, traveled within a few feet of the relocation center fence. (Courtesy National Park Service, Manzanar National Historic Site.)

Past the entrance and police sentry posts was Manzanar's "main street," or First Street, shown here. The town hall and main post office are at left. The police station, *Manzanar Free Press* office, public works division, and other offices are across the street. (Ansel Adams photograph, courtesy Library of Congress Prints and Photographs Division, LC-A351-3-M-27.)

Established as a branch of the Los Angeles Post Office, the Manzanar Post Office began service soon after the camp opened and eventually included five substations. Three carriers delivered mail daily to the barracks apartments. Incoming mail averaged 1,500 letters and 350 parcels each day. In the first months, military police opened and inspected parcels in the presence of the internees receiving them. (War Relocation Authority photograph, courtesy National Archives, NWDNS-210-G-16.)

The first internee-produced newspaper in the 10 camps, the *Manzanar Free Press* began publication on April 11, 1942, with four mimeographed sheets. It grew to an eight-page newspaper with copy and layout prepared in its First Street office, seen above and at right. Chalfant Press, publisher of the Owens Valley's newspapers, printed the paper in Lone Pine. Issei residents charged that the paper catered to younger, English-speaking Nisei until the War Relocation Authority authorized publication of a Japanese supplement in June 1943. Editors insisted that the *Free Press* was an open forum and did not speak for the administration, but they omitted news of the riot on December 6, 1942, that left two internees dead. (Above, courtesy Archie Miyatake, Toyo Miyatake Collection; right, Ansel Adams photograph, Library of Congress Prints and Photographs Division, LC-A35-4-M-4.)

Four internee mounted policemen—and their horses, Bobby, Ginger, Slipper, and Peter—patrolled daily in the summer in the vicinity of the Bairs Creek picnic grounds to keep peace and make certain that residents returned to camp. They were part of an internal police force of approximately 90 internees headed by a Caucasian chief and four lieutenants. (Courtesy Archie Miyatake, Toyo Miyatake Collection.)

The internee police force was responsible for security inside the camp, but some internees refused to cooperate with them and occasionally made threats against them. The policemen were trained in criminal investigation and patrol work, and they wore uniforms made in the camp's garment factory. (War Relocation Authority Collection, courtesy UCLA Special Collections.)

Standing before Manzanar's two pumper trucks are some of the 30 internee firemen who staffed the Manzanar Fire Station in three daily shifts. Headed by a fire chief and three Caucasian captains, and helped out by 34 volunteers, they responded to nearly 100 fires over three years. Most were small brush, kitchen, and electrical fires. (Courtesy Archie Miyatake, Toyo Miyatake Collection.)

Manzanar's only large fire, on July 28, 1944, destroyed three warehouses. Driven by a strong south wind, it resisted the efforts of firefighters—including these off-duty internee firemen and volunteers—and threatened nearby barracks. Block fire brigades, formed the year before, helped residents wet down roofs. Wide, sandy firebreaks separated every two blocks, preventing a larger conflagration in the highly flammable camp. (Courtesy County of Inyo, Eastern California Museum.)

The Public Works Division, responsible for utility and maintenance operations, employed more than 500 internee and WRA personnel, including this office group, shown in 1943 in front of their First Street headquarters. Water diverted from nearby Shepherd Creek into a concrete-lined reservoir flowed into the living area at the rate of 1.5 million gallons daily. Pipelines carried sewage 1.5 miles east, under the Los Angeles Aqueduct, and into a state-of-the-art treatment and water-filtering plant operated by an internee chemist and six assistants under a WRA supervisor. Internee workers also collected 9 tons of garbage daily from garbage can racks installed near the mess halls; much of the food waste went to the hog farm. A crew of 19 crushed tin cans, and 16 more internees collected and processed over 1,500 pounds of grease monthly; both went for war use. (Courtesy Mary Nomura Collection, Manzanar National Historic Site.)

A line crew is shown working on an electrical connection to a barracks. Few internee workers came to Manzanar with experience in construction and maintenance trades. Trained by appointed personnel, they learned surveying, drafting, carpentering, plumbing, and boiler and pump operating. (Ansel Adams photograph, courtesy Library of Congress Prints and Photographs Division, LC-A351-3-M-23-B.)

Workers clear brush by the barbed-wire fence. A few feet away, cars traveling on U.S. Highway 395 often slowed to peer into the camp. From inside, recalled one internee, the highway was "within your reach . . . after three and a half years, you [began] to wonder what it feels like to ride on that highway." (Courtesy Archie Miyatake, Toyo Miyatake Collection.)

With loudspeakers blaring 1940s swing music, teams of workers on the Camouflage Net Project, seen above, weave burlap strips through huge nets hung on frames in three large sheds. The 500 workers employed in the project from June to December 1942 produced an average 6,000 nets a month for the military, with a one-day record of 14 nets set by a Bainbridge Island boys crew. "There was a great sense of camaraderie," said one worker about her team of mostly young workers. Below, crews ride in trucks back to their barracks. Considered war work, employment was open only to citizens. Workers earned $16 a month, far less than weavers on the outside. (Both War Relocation Authority photographs by Dorothea Lange, courtesy National Archives; above, NWDNS-210-G-C815, below, NWDNS-210-G-C810.)

The Manzanar Guayule Rubber Project, sponsored by the California Institute of Technology, gave Japanese American scientists in the camps the opportunity to work on vital defense research. The organizer of the project, faculty member Dr. Robert Emerson, is shown with team members (above) inspecting young guayule plants. Nearly 40 internee nurserymen successfully propagated guayule plants from cuttings in beds and lath houses in the camp's southwest corner. In labs set up in the hospital and Block 6 ironing room (below), chemists, including Frank Hirosawa, developed new and faster methods of extracting high-quality rubber from the plants. (Above, War Relocation Authority photograph by Dorothea Lange, courtesy National Archives, NWDNS-210-G-C724; below, Ansel Adams photograph, Library of Congress Prints and Photographs Division, LC-A35-M-37-A.)

Large-scale agriculture figured prominently in War Relocation Authority plans to make Manzanar as self-sufficient as possible, but with only one rented tractor available at first, the WRA brought in mules that understood Japanese commands. (War Relocation Authority photograph, courtesy National Archives, NWDNS-210-G-C747.)

Internee crews reconditioned 8 miles of irrigation ditches left from Manzanar's farming period and cleared and leveled nearly 500 acres of fields for vegetables and feed crops. Shown here is a new canal in the South Farm Field. Farmers experimented with dozens of vegetables and settled on 32 varieties they could successfully grow in Manzanar's soil. (War Relocation Authority photograph, courtesy National Archive, NWDNS-210-G-C765.)

Farmworkers, including women, are shown in this section of a panoramic photograph. One hundred farm workers walked off the job in June 1942 to protest the use of Caucasian foremen, most not experienced in farming, as escorts in the fields outside camp. Eventually the WRA allowed the farmers to work unescorted under internee foremen. (Courtesy Manzanar National Historic Site.)

Manzanar farmers grew, among others, squash, peppers, eggplant, and string beans, together with daikon, *uri*, *kaboucha*, and several varieties of herbs, onions, and melons. Fourteen tons of tomatoes harvested in 1943 went to an Anaheim, California, cannery for processing. Approximately 10 percent of the yearly farm crop was shipped to other camps. (Ansel Adams photograph, courtesy Library of Congress Prints and Photographs Division, LC-A35-3-M-14.)

The hog farm a mile south of the camp produced more than 300,000 pounds of pork from just over 2,000 hogs fed almost entirely on mess-hall garbage. A beef cattle project, with nearly 400 head, closed down after a year when supplementary feed proved too costly. (Ansel Adams photograph, courtesy Library of Congress Prints and Photographs Division, LC-A351-3-M-31.)

Under the expert care of Manzanar's internee orchard crew, the neglected apple and pear orchards of Manzanar's fruit-growing community produced 4,000 crates of Bartlett and Winter Nellis pears and 600 lugs of Newtown Pippin and Winesap apples in 1942. Foreman Takeo Shima observed "some very fine trees" in the orchards. The camp's newspaper urged residents to "resist temptation and not pick the fruits." (Courtesy Laws Railroad Museum and Historic Site.)

A crew of 28 internees collected eggs each day at 3:30 p.m. at the poultry farm just outside the southwest boundary fence. It had brooder and laying houses for 12,000 hens, together with warehouses, offices, lawns, and flower gardens. Over two years, poultry workers also killed and dressed nearly 9,000 meat birds. This crew is shown delivering fresh poultry to the mess halls. (Courtesy Archie Miyatake, Toyo Miyatake Collection.)

Local residents took notice of Manzanar's large farm fields and gardens. Displays of farm produce, such as this one at Chalfant Press in Lone Pine, helped dispel local hostility toward the camp. Farm output for 1943 was 1,666 tons of vegetables, fruit, and grain, with nearly all of it used in the mess halls. (War Relocation Authority Collection, courtesy UCLA Special Collections.)

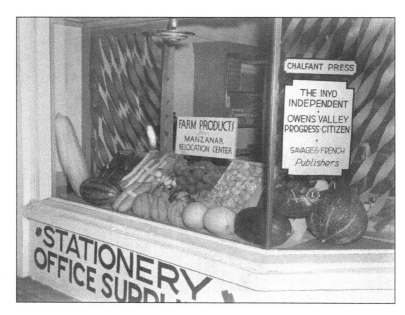

Among the lowest-paid internees, the 1,500 kitchen workers were predominately older Issei and Kibei (American-born Japanese educated in Japan and viewed by administration as potential troublemakers). Mess halls became flash points of internee dissension and resistance. In late 1942, Kibei Harry Ueno organized the Kitchen Workers' Union. It clashed with the pro-administration Japanese American Citizens League and accused WRA personnel of pilfering rationed sugar and meat intended for internees. After the arrest and jailing of Ueno for the beating of another internee, hundreds of his supporters gathered in protest at the Block 22 mess hall on December 6, 1942. The crowd later marched on the police station, precipitating the Manzanar riot that left two internees dead. (Both War Relocation Authority photographs, courtesy National Archives; left, NWDNS0210-G-B119, below, NWDNS-210-G-C889.)

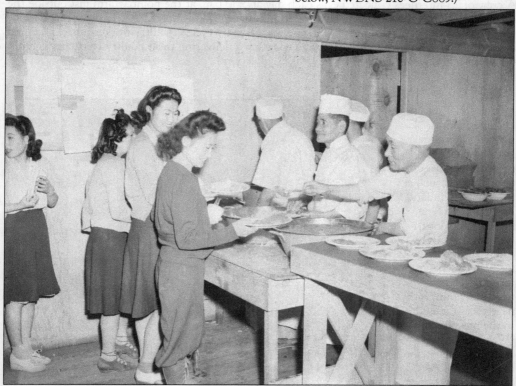

Internees could buy clothing, toys, and sewing supplies at the General Store (above). When new dress materials arrived, the *Manzanar Free Press* reported, women would "push, grab, shove, and turn the store into a bedlam." The Manzanar Cooperative Enterprises also operated a popular canteen that sold newspapers, magazines, smoking supplies, and non-rationed food items. In its first two days of operation, residents bought over 8,000 bottles of lukewarm soda pop. More than 100 internees worked in the co-op's stores, administration, and warehouses (below). (Both Ansel Adams photographs, courtesy Library of Congress Prints and Photographs Division; above, LC-A35-6-M-40; below, LC-A351-3-M-21.)

Thirty internee carpenters and craftsmen, some shown here, worked in the furniture shop turning out nearly 7,000 items for camp use, including desks, chairs, filing cabinets, food trays, cribs for the Children's Village, and chairs for school classrooms. At Christmas, the colorful painted toys they crafted from leftover lumber were sold in the general store. (Courtesy Archie Miyatake, Toyo Miyatake Collection.)

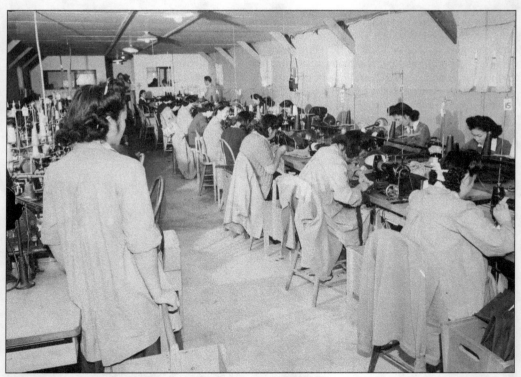

The clothing factory produced hospital uniforms, mess-hall aprons, mattress covers, masks for camouflage net workers, and clothing in all sizes. Started with six home sewing machines, it grew to two warehouses and 100 industrial machines. Internee workers could also train in clothing design, pattern making, cutting, and sewing. (Ansel Adams photograph, courtesy Library of Congress Prints and Photographs Division, LC-A35-5-M-45Bx.)

Internee construction crews started work on the high school auditorium, seen here in February 1944, and completed it in time for the June graduation. The 14,000-square-foot structure had a stage, locker rooms, offices, and a movie-projection booth. Internees also built the WRA staff housing, sentry posts, and additions to many existing buildings. (War Relocation Authority photograph, courtesy National Archives, NWDNS-210-G-G588.)

Ten boiler tenders, including Frank Ukita, who is seen here, watched over these oil-fired boilers that supplied hot water, steam, and heating for the 19-building hospital complex. (War Relocation Authority photograph, courtesy National Archives, NWDNS-210-G-G454.)

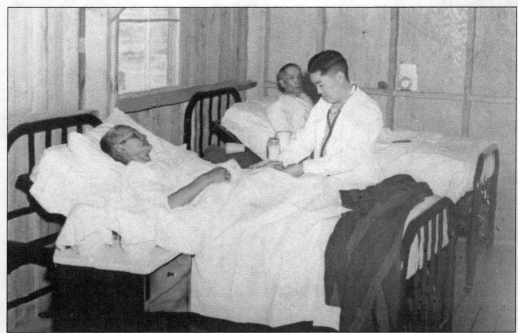

Manzanar's first hospital opened in two rooms and later moved to a three-barracks facility, where Dr. James Goto is shown above treating patients. A Los Angeles County Hospital surgeon, Goto was the first doctor to arrive at Manzanar and headed the medical staff in the camp's first months. Residents took pride in the new 250-bed hospital (below) and its airy wards, gleaming operating rooms, and state-of-the-art equipment. The incidence of serious illness in camp remained low, and the death rate was comparable to that on the outside. Camp life took its toll, however, in widespread psychoneurosis, hypertension, and peptic ulcers. (Above, War Relocation Authority photograph, courtesy National Archives, NWDNS-B150; below, Sato Collection, Manzanar National Historic Site.)

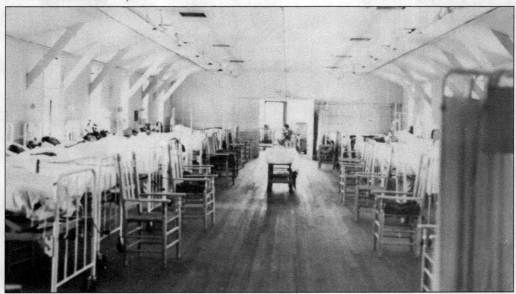

Four internee dentists and 11 assistants saw an average of 60 to 70 patients daily at the dental clinic's main office at the hospital and a branch in Block 7. (Courtesy Archie Miyatake, Toyo Miyatake Collection.)

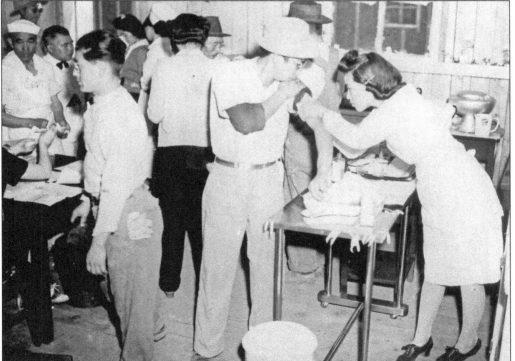

Disease prevention was a priority in the densely populated camp. Within the first month, medical staff administered typhoid inoculations to all incoming internees. (War Relocation Authority photograph, courtesy National Archives, NWDNS-210-G-B98.)

These Issei landscapers and gardeners, including Toyoshigi Ioki (right), carried out extensive landscaping at the new hospital, planting lawns and flower beds, transplanting trees from other parts of camp, and building terracing and rock gardens. Stonemason Ryozo Kado designed rock benches in his signature faux-wood style and created a large pond garden to complement the landscaping. (Courtesy Archie Miyatake, Toyo Miyatake Collection.)

Internee photographer Toyo Miyatake captured the stark beauty of winter at Manzanar in this scene looking toward the General Store. (Courtesy Archie Miyatake, Toyo Miyatake Collection.)

Six

MAKING THE BEST OF IT

More essential than the luggage Japanese Americans carried into Manzanar was their response to sudden confinement: "shikata ga ni," or "it cannot be helped." Most chose to go on with life: they fell in love, succeeded in school, worked productively, had fun, and learned new skills. "The threads of normal life that were broken with the evacuation were slowly mending," wrote the *Manzanar Free Press.* To people accustomed to work and activity, the enforced idleness and boredom of early camp life were, for many, more difficult to bear than the primitive barracks and inedible food. It was no surprise, then, that from the beginning, internees took the camp's urgent needs into their own hands when they could, and those with skills and talents stepped forward to help make the best of a very bad situation. Volunteer teachers started nursery schools, gardeners planted lawns, restaurant chefs helped set up mess halls, and doctors and nurses organized a hospital. Leisure-time activities gave morale a lift as well, and a WRA Community Activities section employed 150 internees who supervised arts and crafts, athletics, gardening, music, the Boy Scouts, and social events. Weekly Sunday night Concerts Under the Stars brought out 1,000 or more classical music lovers who gathered in the south firebreak and listened to selections from records played by internee Harry Ushyjima. Nearly 3,000 adults took Americanization classes and courses in English, history, science, and sewing during 1942, and while many internees turned to church-going, others "made the best of it" by distilling prohibited rice gin in their barracks. Devoted fishermen found the Sierra Nevada's nearby streams irresistible and regularly crawled under the barbed-wire fence with rods and reels in hand. More than any other activity, though, baseball brought the excitement, competition, and identity with America that many internees yearned for. When the Aces, Scorpions, Broncos, or Gophers played, anticipation built and thousands came to watch at the field near Block 19. "Softball governs," wrote the *Manzanar Free Press,* "150 teams rule supreme."

By the first summer, more than 100 men's and 14 women's softball teams were playing on fields carved into Manzanar's firebreaks. Shown here are members of the Dusty Chicks team from Los Angeles, one of several that came intact from their prewar communities. Most older Issei men had never played baseball, but at Manzanar ,they formed their own league with three teams. (War Relocation Authority photograph, courtesy National Archives, NWDS-210-G-D527.)

As barracks were going up, baseball players of all ages played sandlot games in the bulldozed blocks. The number-one sport at Manzanar, baseball brought excitement to an often monotonous camp life and was a symbol of the America most internees still believed in. "Putting on a baseball uniform was like wearing the American flag," said one. (War Relocation Authority photograph, courtesy National Archives, NWDNS-210-G-B134.)

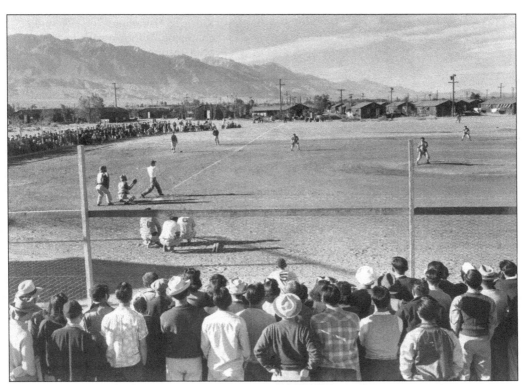

By 1943, Manzanar had its own major-league-size field with a backstop, announcer's stand, and bleachers. Crowds of 2,000 or more, including WRA employees and their families, came to cheer on the Scorpions, ManzaKnights, Yankees, Has-Beens, and other teams in the weekend games. Issei men, among the most avid fans, placed bets on their favorites. To control dust on windy days, the Manzanar Fire Department used its hoses to water down the field before play got started. At right, the Tamura brothers played on the legendary prewar San Fernando Aces team. At Manzanar, players sent for their uniforms and began practice. The Aces swept most games and held the Manzanar National League crown. (Above, Ansel Adams photograph, courtesy Library of Congress Prints and Photographs Division, LC-A351-3-M-6; right, National Park Service, Manzanar National Historic Site.)

Kuniyaki Sakamoto, the 1944 judo champion, is shown with instructor Shig Tashima, one of nearly 100 black belt holders at Manzanar. More than 400 men and boys participated in judo, practicing up to five times weekly and competing in monthly tournaments. Internee builders later enclosed the open sawdust-and-canvas judo platform, creating a traditionally styled judo dojo, or hall. (Courtesy Rosie Maruki Kakuuchi Collection, Manzanar National Historic Site.)

The Venice Barbell Club, seen here, reportedly held the title of strongest Japanese barbell club in the United States before going to Manzanar. Other weight-lifting teams at camp included the Mayors, Southern Cal, and Westelaye. The teams competed in regular meets until some of their members relocated out of camp. (Courtesy County of Inyo, Eastern California Museum.)

The Manzanar Golf Club grew to 150 golfing enthusiasts and three internee instructors employed by the WRA. In the camp's southwest corner, they laid out a nine-hole golf course of compacted and oiled sand; later enlarged to 18 holes, it was the scene of monthly tournaments. At the March 1944 meet, winner Susumu Katsuda shot a 60 in 18 holes. (War Relocation Authority photograph, courtesy National Archives, NWDNS-210-G-B219.)

The Buckeyes, Bel-Aires, and Dusty Nine were among the girl's teams playing volleyball at the sports center, where basketball and tennis courts were also available. Workers brought in clay-like soil from the Owens River to surface the four tennis courts. (Ansel Adams photograph, courtesy Library of Congress Prints and Photographs Division, LC-A35-6-M-14.)

Blooms for this flower-arranging exhibit at the Visual Education Museum came from internees' gardens and the camp's nursery. Internee curators and craftsmen mounted a full schedule of exhibits about woodcraft, children's art, wartime rationing, Hollywood movies, and other topics. (Courtesy Archie Miyatake, Toyo Miyatake Collection.)

Internee artists offered classes in watercolor and oil painting soon after the camp opened. Eventually more than 40 internee instructors taught drawing, stenciling, embroidery, paper flower making, *ikebana* (flower arranging), and Japanese brush painting. Especially popular for men were classes in model airplane building and woodcraft using old tree roots. (War Relocation Authority photograph by Dorothea Lange, courtesy National Archives, NWDNS-210-G-C897.)

Many internees, mainly Issei, turned to gardening for recreation and morale building (above). More than 120 families rented plots in the South Firebreak Victory Garden for a monthly fee of 35¢ or less. Residents of entire blocks tended larger communal plots. As depicted in the Japanese edition of the *Manzanar Free Press* below, internees found satisfaction in growing their own vegetables and flowers. They gave most of what they grew to the general store to sell, with proceeds going to recreational activities. (Above, War Relocation Authority photograph by Dorothea Lange, courtesy National Archives NWDNS-210-G-C677; below, National Park Service, Manzanar National Historic Site.)

In the first chaotic weeks, with no government plans yet in place for educating Manzanar's 2,500 school-age children, internee teachers organized a preschool program for those ages three to six. By the fall, 1,000 children were attending 18 nursery school classes and seven kindergartens. Teachers emphasized health, safety, social and emotional adjustment, and use of English. (War Relocation Authority photograph, courtesy National Archives, NWDNS-210-G-A918.)

By summer, administrators later recalled, children were "running wild." As parents clamored for a school, the WRA organized a voluntary summer education program. Classes started in late June with few classrooms and no supplies or experienced teachers. Nearly 1,000 students enrolled and 50 internee tutors took charge of all 12 grades. Most classes were held outside in the shade of barracks. (War Relocation Authority photograph by Dorothea Lange, courtesy National Archives, NWDNS-210-G-C665.)

Mrs. Whiteacre's fourth-grade class, seen above in 1945, is in costume for a school pageant. By then, the elementary school, its classes previously scattered in 12 blocks throughout camp, was consolidated in Block 16. Curriculum was "like that of any other progressive California school which emphasizes the social studies program," wrote superintendent of schools Genevieve Carter. Manzanar schoolchildren did not escape yearly standardized testing, in which they "reached or exceeded the national norms," and were especially strong "in spelling and arithmetic computation," Carter reported. Below, classes leave school for a fire drill. (Above, courtesy County of Inyo, Eastern California Museum; below, Archie Miyatake, Toyo Miyatake Collection.)

The high school glee club, seen here on the auditorium stage in 1945, brought music to Manzanar with Christmas concerts, oratorios, and stage productions, including "Ballad for Americans," performed at the 1943 graduation. Popular music teacher Louis Frizzell, at left, directed the group and composed music for its performances. (Courtesy Archie Miyatake, Toyo Miyatake Collection.)

Classes for nearly 1,400 high school students got under way on October 15, 1942, in Block 7. Supervised by Caucasian teachers, internee student teachers took over some classes, including this one in chemistry, seen here in 1943. Students came from over 200 high schools, but they gradually formed a student body with a student government, newspaper, and dozens of clubs. (Ansel Adams photograph, courtesy Library of Congress Prints and Photographs Division, LC-A35-5-M-32.)

Inscriptions in this yearbook are to 1943 summer graduate Mary Kageyama, known as the "Songbird of Manzanar." A talented and popular singer, she starred in high school musicals and entertained at dances and parties with her renditions of popular 1940s hits. With school time lost during the removal, students could graduate in March or June in 1943. (Courtesy Mary Nomura and County of Inyo, Eastern California Museum.)

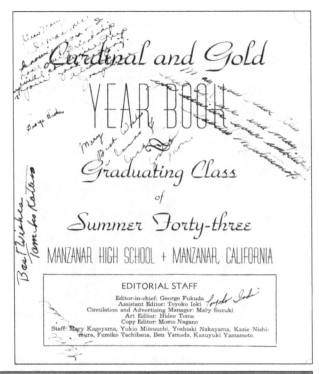

With 1,200 family members and friends looking on, 177 Manzanar high school seniors received their diplomas in the newly completed auditorium on June 18, 1944. Five types were offered: general, college entrance, commercial, homemaking, and agriculture. Graduates attending college reportedly achieved better than average success. (Courtesy Archie Miyatake, Toyo Miyatake Collection.)

A tropical theme set the scene for the 1945 spring formal dance. The camp celebrated most holidays with a dance, usually accompanied by entertainment and refreshments. The popular weekend movie nights typically filled the huge auditorium to capacity. (Courtesy Archie Miyatake, Toyo Miyatake Collection.)

The popular Jive Bombers swing band played for dances and musical shows. Other musicians formed a salon orchestra, mandolin and guitar group, community orchestra, and the Sierra Stars, a hillbilly band that featured washboards and pans. (Ansel Adams photograph, War Relocation Authority Collection, courtesy UCLA Special Collections.)

In confinement, many younger, Americanized internees participated for the first time in the traditional Japanese activities of their parents and grandparents, including Japanese music and dancing. Singers and musicians practiced the *shamisen*, *shakuhachi*, *koto*, and other instruments and performed often in traditional dress (above). Depicted in this *Manzanar Free Press* drawing, (below), block residents rehearsed *ondo* dancing weeks in advance of the annual summer Obon Festival sponsored by the Buddhist church. (Above, courtesy Archie Miyatake, Toyo Miyatake Collection; below, courtesy National Park Service, Manzanar National Historic Site.)

Ondo practice in Block 30.

Queen of the 1943 Fall Fair Diane Tani is at far left in this photograph with her court. Pictured from left to right are Amy Iwaki, Kiyo Yoshida, Mae Kageyama, and Yoneko Kodama. The two-day fair featured farm, garden, craft, and industrial exhibits as well as musical entertainment and a coronation ball for the royal court. (Courtesy Mae Kakehashi Collection, Manzanar National Historic Site.)

Yoshiko Hosoi (center) and her sister Masuye (left) are seen in front of the administration building as a friend and the young daughter of a War Relocation Authority employee enjoy ice cream on a hot day. (Courtesy Isao Sakurai for the Yoshiko Sakurai Collection, Manzanar National Historic Site.)

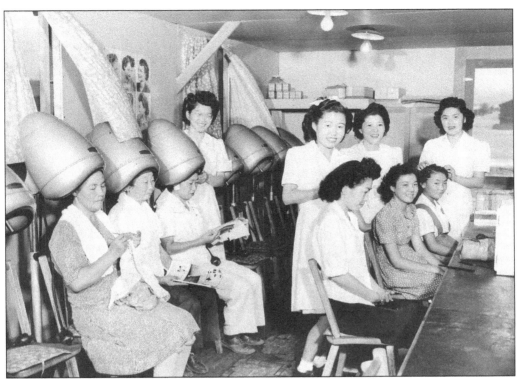

At the beauty parlor in Block 15, residents could get shampoos, haircuts, permanent waves, and a full line of other services at prices below those charged on the outside. Teachers and other women on the WRA staff used the shop as well, paying slightly higher prices. (Courtesy Archie Miyatake, Toyo Miyatake Collection.)

Many Issei preferred more traditional pursuits to joining American-style social activities. Men built tables and chairs in recreation halls for playing *goh*, a game of strategy similar to checkers. (War Relocation Authority photograph by Dorothea Lange, courtesy National Archives, NWDNS-210-G-C784.)

Most children carried only a favorite doll or small toy when they left home to go to Manzanar, and wartime shortages made buying toys difficult in camp. Teachers set up a toy loan library, where children could check out wagons, balls, puzzles, and other toys for a week. Children are shown lining up to return their toys. (Courtesy Archie Miyatake, Toyo Miyatake Collection.)

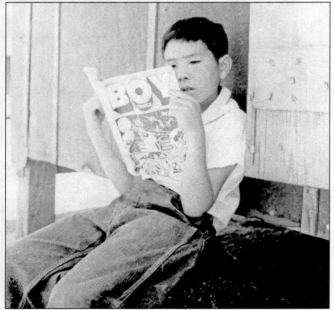

Readers of all ages checked out books and magazines from one of Manzanar's libraries. The first opened in May 1942, with 1,000 discarded books from the Los Angeles Public Library. Others included a main branch, elementary and high school libraries, and a fiction branch. (War Relocation Authority photograph by Dorothea Lange, courtesy National Archives, NWDNS-210-G-C893.)

At the Manzanar hospital, student nurses could continue training programs interrupted by the removal. Here they receive their caps from chief nurse Jacquelyn Hawes. Many went on to nursing careers after camp. (Courtesy Archie Miyatake, Toyo Miyatake Collection.)

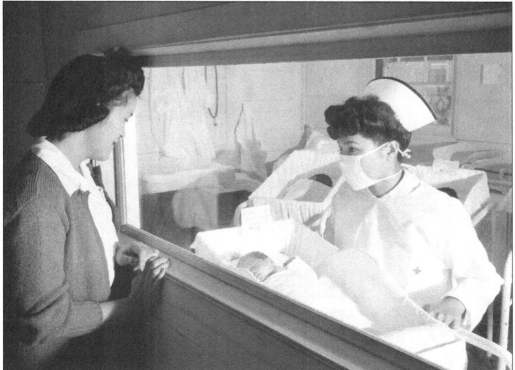

Manzanar's first baby, Kenji Ogawa, was born, according to the *Manzanar Free Press*, when "the stork, which had been hovering over the village for several days, decided to alight April 16 [1942]." Nurse Aiko Hamaguchi holds one of the other 540 babies born at Manzanar. (Ansel Adams photograph, courtesy Library of Congress Prints and Photographs Division, LC-A35-5-M-4.)

Seated in front of one of the camp's three Buddhist church locations are members 70 years and older honored at the Pioneer Day service and festivities in the fall of 1942. With them is Rev. Shinjo Nagatomi, director of the Shinsu, or First Buddhist, congregation and its activities. An August 1942 religious census showed 4,048 Buddhists, or almost half the camp population then.

Later that year, nearly 1,900 persons attended weekly services. Suspicions of Buddhists' allegiance to Japan persisted, but the Young Buddhist Association and other groups were among the most community-minded in camp. (Courtesy Isao Sakurai, Yoshiko Sakurai Collection, Manzanar National Historic Site.)

Fr. Leo Steinbach greets parishioners at St. Francis Xavier Catholic Church in Block 25. With fewer than 500 members, it was the smallest of the camp's religious groups but reportedly was the most closely knit. The church received more than 250 converts at Manzanar. Pictured also are Sisters Mary Bernadette and Mary Suzanna, Japanese Maryknoll nuns who assisted at the church. (Ansel Adams photograph, courtesy Library of Congress Prints and Photographs Division, LC-A351-T01-3-M-2.)

Romance continued to bloom at Manzanar, and 188 couples were married during the nearly four years of camp. Yuichi (right) and Fumiko Hirata are shown here after their wedding on April 2, 1943, at the Manzanar Christian Church in Block 15. A reception and dance followed in the Block 27 mess hall. (Courtesy County of Inyo, Eastern California Museum.)

Like most cities, Manzanar had places of escape from crowded living, and Merritt Park (above) was Manzanar's "city park." Its nearly half an acre of tranquility included two lakes connected by a waterfall and a teahouse that overlooked the water. Nurseryman Kuichiro Nishi planted dozens of rosebushes, giving the park its original name of Rose Park. From certain places within the park, barracks and guard towers were out of sight, making it a favorite place for photographs. An outing at rustic Bairs Creek (below), flowing through the camp's southwest corner, was a welcome escape from summer heat. Internees created a picnic area, with tables, barbecues, and trails and issued permits to limit use. (Above, Ansel Adams photograph, courtesy Library of Congress Prints and Photographs Division, LC-A351-3-M-11; below, War Relocation Authority photograph by Dorothea Lange, National Archives, NWDNS-210-G-C793.)

Seven

TAKING LEAVE

From the time the uprooted people of Japanese ancestry arrived at Manzanar, the day of their departure was not far from their minds. For all its industries and activities, camp life seemed stagnant and without a definable future. "Life in Manzanar is easy, but it isn't living; life out here isn't easy, but it's life in America," wrote one relocated student. Young people seized opportunities to move forward with their lives, and many left to attend college or take jobs in the Midwest or East. Yet many older internees held back on departure plans, fearful of lingering hostility on the outside and reluctant to start over in a strange place. Certainly no one wanted to die in camp behind barbed wire and far from home, but the lives of 150 men, women, children, and infants did end at Manzanar, including two young men shot by military police in the December 1942 riot.

The roads out of camp gradually opened, but all pointed east, away from former homes and the West Coast military areas that would remain closed to Japanese Americans until early 1945. Furlough programs allowed internees to leave for short periods of work in other states, and in late 1942, the first Manzanar volunteers were inducted into the U.S. Army.

In the aftermath of the riot, authorities removed Kibei and Issei leaders and agitators to isolation centers in Arizona and Utah, while the WRA took their pro-administration Nisei adversaries and their families, 65 in all, to safety in Death Valley. A registration program in February 1943, intended to determine "loyalty" and identify internees eligible for resettlement, instead divided families and sent tensions soaring. "No" answers to the ambiguous "loyalty" Question 28 on the long questionnaire branded those respondents "disloyal." Most, together with their families, were transferred to Tule Lake Segregation Center in Northern California. As eligible internees relocated in greater numbers in 1943 and 1944, the camp population declined, and with the lifting of the West Coast exclusion order in December 1944, Manzanar's residents were free to return to their homes. The last internees left Manzanar on November 21, 1945.

Elaborate floral displays softened the barracks surroundings at most Manzanar funerals, including this service for 48-year-old Issei Tono Myose on December 31, 1943, at the Buddhist church. A camp flower shop fashioned many of the displays, using artificial blooms or seasonal fresh flowers from barracks gardens or Victory Garden plots. (Courtesy Rose Honda Collection, Manzanar National Historic Site.)

The death of Matsunosuke Murakami at age 62, on May 16, 1942, was the first of 150 in camp, but his grave, seen here, was one of only 15 burials in the Manzanar cemetery. Most were infants and premature newborns or, like Murakami, older adults with no known relatives in camp. After Manzanar closed, all but six remains were removed to other cemeteries. (War Relocation Authority photograph by Dorothea Lange, courtesy National Archives, NWDNS-210-G-C902.)

As life at Manzanar lengthened into prolonged confinement, internees and administration had to plan for the deaths that would inevitably occur. They selected a cemetery site at the camp's western edge, outside the barbed-wire fence and within an old peach orchard from the area's fruit-growing period. Residents and clergy asked master stonemason Ryozo Kado to build a permanent monument for the cemetery. Known for his stonework grottoes at Catholic churches in the Los Angeles area, Kado designed this tall white obelisk, shown here in 1991, and collected a few cents from each internee to cover the $1,000 cost of construction. The Japanese characters read *I Rei To*, meaning "soul consoling tower." Most of the 150 people who died in camp were cremated, according to Japanese and Buddhist tradition, and their remains kept in urns in the Buddhist church or the hospital until the camp closed. (Photograph by author.)

Akiko Hosoi, left, and her sister Yoshiko are pictured ready to leave Manzanar for Iowa, where Akiko attended Grinnell College. Supported by camp administrators and the National Student Relocation Program, more than 4,000 college-age students from relocations centers went to colleges and universities in the Midwest and East. (Courtesy Isao Sakurai, Yoshiko Sakurai Collection, Manzanar National Historic Site.)

Facing wartime labor shortages, western sugar beet growers appealed to the WRA for internee help harvesting the beet crop. Companies sent recruiters to Manzanar during the summer, and within two weeks, nearly 1,000 mostly male internees had been granted work furloughs and were on their way to Utah, Idaho, Colorado, and Montana. This appreciation letter later appeared in the *Manzanar Free Press*. (Courtesy National Park Service, Manzanar National Historic Site.)

MONDAY, NOV. 31, 1942   MANZANAR FREE PRESS   PAGE THREE

We thank the
VOLUNTEER WORKERS
from Manzanar

RESPONSE from Manzanar for volunteer workers to help save the sugar beets in territory served by the factories of this company was especially good.
About nine hundred volunteers from this center have this fall served the sugar beet growers of our territory and have thereby served America. An additional hundred or so have gone to other sugar growing areas or to other farm work.

WHILE the overall response from the 110,000 evacuees in all relocation centers has not been what was originally hoped for either by farmers or evacuees themselves, there are some very hopeful signs for the future.
Owing to the emergency conditions under which the entire program of private recruiting and employment of evacuees was carried on during the past season some mistakes were made on both sides. However, the fair treatment received generally by these volunteer workers from employers and their neighbors, and the splendid service performed by the workers, have combined to create a better understanding of this difficult problem and form a foundation to build on for the future we confidently look forward to an even closer cooperation between farmers and evacuees in 1943.

AMERICA needs more beet sugar. Thirty states are now wholly dependent upon sugar from this industry and from two Pacific Coast cane refineries, while six additional states need large quantities of beet sugar to make up their deficiency supply. You can serve America well by joining the 'army of harvesters' who are helping to increase the nation's food supplies.

Plan now to 'join up' next spring
UTAH-IDAHO SUGAR CO.

With internment increasingly difficult to justify on the grounds of military necessity, the WRA and army initiated a registration program in February 1943 to assess internee loyalty. Here army recruiters explain registration to draft-age males. Internees were asked if they would serve in combat and swear unqualified allegiance to the United States. Affirmative answers cleared the way for draft eligibility or application for "indefinite leave." By war's end, 42 volunteers and 132 draftees had been inducted into the army from Manzanar, including these men being sworn in at a ceremony in Block 16 mess hall (below). (Above, War Relocation Authority photograph, courtesy National Archives NWDNS-210-G; below, Japanese American Archive, Special Collections and Archives, California State University Sacramento.)

Nisei men in uniform returning to Manzanar on leave were a familiar sight in 1944. In barracks windows, families displayed the service banners seen in many American homes, with a star for each son or daughter in the armed forces. A United Service Organization (USO) canteen, set up in a barracks, hosted parties and entertainment for the soldiers. Most who had volunteered or were drafted from Manzanar joined the combined 442nd Regimental Combat Team/100th Infantry Battalion, an all-Nisei unit that saw combat in North Africa, France, and Italy. It suffered 9,486 casualties and was the most highly decorated unit in the U.S. Army. Other Nisei with Japanese language skills were recruited for the Military Intelligence Service. Trained in Minnesota and attached to combat units in the Pacific as scouts and translators, they were credited with saving thousands of American lives. (Courtesy Archie Miyatake, Toyo Miyatake Collection.)

Mourners watch as the flag is lowered following a joint memorial service for Sgt. Robert Nakasaki and Pfc. Sadao Munemori, whose families were interned at Manzanar. Both died in Italy on April 5, 1945. The only Japanese American awarded the Medal of Honor during World War II, Private First Class Munemori received it posthumously for saving fellow soldiers when he threw himself on a grenade. (Courtesy Archie Miyatake, Toyo Miyatake Collection.)

Kay Fukuda, on leave at Manzanar in this photograph, was one of nearly 200 young Japanese American women who entered nurse's training from the relocation centers by enlisting in the U.S. Cadet Nurse's Corps program. (Ansel Adams photograph, courtesy Library of Congress Prints and Photographs Division, LC-A35-4-M-69.)

In February 1944, the War Relocation Authority transferred 1,876 Manzanar internees to Tule Lake Segregation Center in Northern California. The group seen above carries luggage to a waiting train at Lone Pine Station. It included persons desiring repatriation to Japan and others determined to be "disloyal," those who had answered "no" to the registration's Question 28 that asked them to foreswear allegiance to Japan. Obligated by cultural tradition to keep families intact, many "loyal," Americanized Nisei accompanied their Issei and Kibei family members into segregation. In all, nearly 2,200 Manzanar internees spent the remainder of the war at Tule Lake, occupying an area known as "Manzanar." Baseball players kept their former camp identity, too, when they formed this team, seen below. (Above, War Relocation Authority Collection, courtesy UCLA Special Collections; below, Japanese American Archive, Special Collections and Archives, California State University Sacramento.)

Promotional campaigns by the WRA in late 1944 and 1945 persuaded more than 500 Manzanar internees to relocate to Seabrook, New Jersey, where jobs awaited them in the Seabrook Farms cannery and dehydration plant. Here residents and WRA personnel wave farewell to friends aboard a "Seabrook Special" bus, part of a group that left in March 1945. (War Relocation Authority Collection, courtesy UCLA Special Collections.)

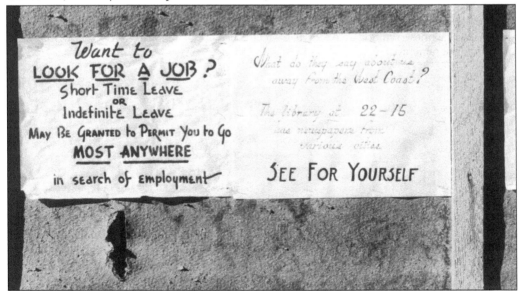

With proof of an employment offer or other means of support, and evidence they would be accepted in their new community, eligible internees could apply for indefinite leave and relocate east of the West Coast exclusion area. At meetings like this one, they could learn about jobs and attitudes toward Japanese in other parts of the country. (Ansel Adams photograph, courtesy Library of Congress Prints and Photographs Division, LC-A35-4-M-2.)

Gateway to relocation.

In the *Manzanar Free Press* Japanese edition graphic seen above, the camp entrance is depicted as the "gateway to relocation" in an effort to encourage Issei resettlement. Below, a WRA van with departing internees leaves Manzanar. As the relocation program moved forward, the Manzanar population became predominantly older adults and those under 20, and the rate of departures declined. Issei in particular, handicapped by age and health concerns, feared leaving the security that Manzanar offered to start over on the outside, far from California. Manzanar, wrote one WRA official, "in its scenic setting, with its grounds becoming more and more pleasant, was an ideal old men's home." (Above, courtesy National Park Service, Manzanar National Historic Site; below, Japanese American Archive, Special Collections and Archives, California State University Sacramento.)

With no direct train connection from Manzanar to cities east of the exclusion zone, relocating internees traveled at first by commercial bus to trains leaving from Reno, Nevada. When they encountered harassment from other passengers, the WRA put an 11-passenger van into service, seen here. (Ansel Adams photograph, courtesy Library of Congress Prints and Photographs Division, LC-351-6-M-55.)

The *Manzanar Free Press* described WRA escort and local resident Nan Zischank as a "companion, guide, advisor, and diplomat." Shown here with her husband, Max, she drove the relocating internees to Reno three times weekly. From 1943 to 1945, she logged, by her own estimate, nearly 170,000 miles in the WRA van she dubbed the "Black Mariah." (Courtesy Nan Zischank Collection.)

Above, internees listen as WRA Community Welfare Director Margaret D'Ille reads the proclamation, dated December 17, 1944, that revoked the West Coast exclusion order and restored internees' rights to return to their former homes. News that the relocation centers would close within a year was met with disbelief by many of the 5,549 people still living at Manzanar. Camp operations began closing down in the summer of 1945, in part to convince residents they could no longer postpone leaving. Schools remained closed after June, and the last issue of the *Manzanar Free Press* appeared on October 19. Below, Manzanar residents leave church in the snow in this 1944 photograph. (Above, courtesy Archie Miyatake, Toyo Miyatake Collection; below, Ansel Adams photograph, courtesy Library of Congress Prints and Photographs Division, LC-A35-6-M-33.)

Wearing a new suit made by her mother, 19-year-old Rosie Maruki poses for a farewell picture before leaving Manzanar in August 1945. In July, Project Director Ralph Merritt announced that Manzanar would close by November 30, and on August 14, Japan surrendered to the Allied forces, ending more than three and a half years of war. As the pace of departures stepped up, internee workers began dismantling the camp. With salvaged lumber, departing internees built shipping crates. Some purchased cars in Lone Pine to avoid taking WRA buses to Los Angeles. Although the WRA encouraged internees to resettle in the eastern states where jobs and housing were more available, most, like Rosie Maruki and her family, wanted to go home to Southern California, even if it meant living temporarily in crowded trailer camps, hostels, or group homes. (Courtesy Rosie Maruki Kakuuchi Collection, Manzanar National Historic Site.)

Project director Ralph Merritt speaks informally to WRA personnel as the last internees leave Manzanar at 11:00 a.m. on November 21, 1945. A tearful four-year-old, accompanied by his mother, was the last to walk out the entrance gate, away from the only home he had known. (Courtesy County of Inyo, Eastern California Museum.)

The entrance for Manzanar War Relocation Center became the departure point for everyone who left at the end of four years. (Ansel Adams photograph, courtesy Library of Congress Prints and Photographs Division, LC-A351-3-M-28.)

Eight

LANDSCAPES
OF REMEMBERING

As the last bus of departing internees faded from view, War Relocation Authority personnel turned to the tasks of cleaning out barracks, turning off electrical and water connections, and recording in voluminous final reports all that had happened in the previous four years. By the following year, nearly all of Manzanar's 800 or so buildings were gone, sold whole or as salvage lumber to contractors, local residents, and veterans. A small, temporary community of local veterans and their families lived in the 22 WRA barracks, then called the Manzanar Housing Project. By 1952, the only remaining structures were the auditorium, later converted to an Inyo County maintenance garage, and stonemason Ryozo Kado's two sentry houses and tall white cemetery monument. But scattered about the Owens Valley is Manzanar's legacy, in barracks that became apartments, motels, and social halls and in lumber turned into homes, businesses, fences, and sheds. Water pipe went to Big Pine, and hospital equipment modernized Bishop's medical care.

As the years passed at Manzanar, garden ponds, latrine slabs, and baseball diamonds disappeared under sand and desert scrub. Locals returned each fall to pick fruit in the struggling orchards, and cattle grazed through Victory Gardens and farm fields. Internees' memories of Manzanar disappeared as well, into a long silence of shame, broken only when a younger generation grew curious about the lost years of family pasts. Two decades or more passed before the stories seldom told could be shared with others. At the same time, former internees began returning to Manzanar, and an organized group pilgrimage in 1969 grew into an annual event that now draws up to 1,000 former residents, families, and visitors. Though not without controversy, a decades-long grassroots efforts aimed at public education, preservation of stories, and increased recognition for Manzanar picked up momentum and culminated in its designation as a National Historic Site in 1992. The "place that's hardly there" is now a place for remembering all of its pasts.

After the last internees departed in November 1945, a reduced WRA staff stayed at Manzanar until the following March, when the General Land Office took over. Later, under the War Assets Administration, its field representative, former Project Director Ralph Merritt, oversaw the sale and demolition of 742 Manzanar buildings through the fall of 1946. Veterans from Inyo County and others outside the area bought 183 barracks that yielded nearly 800,000 board feet of usable lumber. Below, contractors and other buyers were required to move or dismantle the barracks and clean up the land where they had been. This building, later removed to Bishop for use as a church parsonage, was one of 25 used for the Inyo County Housing Project until 1952. (Both courtesy National Park Service, Manzanar National Historic Site.)

Ready with a snowball is Dolores Persichetti, shown at right in the former WRA staff housing area where she lived with her family in 1946 and 1947. To ease the local postwar housing shortage, apartments and dormitories in the Manzanar Housing Project were made available to local World War II veterans. At one time, up to 60 families reportedly lived in the project. Dolores and other high school students in the project attended school in Independence, and a school bus picked them up at the former camp entrance. As a cheerleader, she led cheers for the school's basketball games, played in the former auditorium-gymnasium. Dolores's mother worked for the War Assets Administration. The staff is shown below near the flagpole of the former administration building, barely visible after a heavy snowfall. (Both courtesy Dolores Pratt.)

The Manzanar site reverted to its owner, the Los Angeles Department of Water and Power (DWP), on April 2, 1947. With the housing project vacant by 1952, the DWP auctioned the former staff barracks. Many are still in use throughout the Owens Valley as social halls, motels, and apartments. Staff employees at the camp once climbed these steps, at left in the 1980s, to enter their apartments. For the next 40 years, Los Angeles leased most of the Manzanar site for cattle grazing. Each fall, local residents harvested apples and pears from the remnant orchards, and windblown sand gradually filled in the camp's elaborate ponds and rock-work gardens, hiding many completely from view. Above, the hospital garden pond is again visible after National Park Service archaeologists excavated it in the 1990s. (Above, courtesy National Park Service, Manzanar National Historic Site; left photograph by author.)

Leased to the Independence Veterans of Foreign Wars from 1946 to 1951, the former relocation center auditorium served local towns as a community theater, social hall, and high school gymnasium. A highlight of those years was the exhibition game played by a traveling team of the Harlem Globetrotters. Time took its toll on the building, seen here around 1996. (Courtesy National Park Service, Manzanar National Historic Site.)

Inyo County converted the former auditorium to a road-equipment maintenance garage after 1952 by replacing the wood floor with concrete and removing the stage for a large vehicle door. The building remained in that use until 1996, when it was purchased by the National Park Service as part of Manzanar National Historic Site. (Courtesy National Park Service, Manzanar National Historic Site.)

Manzanar Buddhist minister Rev. Sentoku Mayeda and his friend Rev. Soichi Wakahiro, a Christian minister, first returned to the Manzanar cemetery on Memorial Day in 1946. By 1969, when 150 younger former internees and others gathered for their own pilgrimage, the elderly ministers had been returning for 24 years. Shown above in 1985, the Manzanar Pilgrimage is now a yearly event and draws hundreds of former internees, families, students, and visitors for a day of remembrance, programs, and interfaith worship. Below, Ross Hopkins, the first National Park Service superintendent at Manzanar, is shown at the 1997 pilgrimage with Manzanar Committee chairwoman Sue Kunitomi Embrey (left) and Advisory Commission member Rose Ochi. Hopkins oversaw early archaeology projects and worked toward acquiring the auditorium for restoration. (Above, courtesy Sato collection, Manzanar National Historic Site; below, Manzanar Committee, Manzanar National Historic Site.)

Former internee Sue Kunitomi Embrey, seen above in the pilgrimage *ondo* dance, led the Manzanar Committee in the effort to gain official recognition for the site. It was designated a California State Landmark in 1972, but wording on the official plaque, in particular the use of "concentration camp" to describe Manzanar, angered veterans' groups, Owens Valley residents, and others. At right, pilgrimage banners honor all 10 relocation centers. With more public education came federal legislation acknowledging that the camps had been a mistake. Signed by Pres. Ronald Reagan on August 10, 1988, it provided payment of $20,000 to every surviving internee. An apology from Pres. George H. W. Bush the following year noted, "A monetary sum and words alone cannot restore lost years." (Above, courtesy Bruce Embrey, the Manzanar Committee; right, courtesy National Park Service, Manzanar National Historic Site.)

On February 19, 1992, the 50th anniversary of Executive Order 9066, Congress designated Manzanar a National Historic Site. In a complex land exchange in 1996, the City of Los Angeles turned over 814 acres to federal ownership, and the National Park Service took custody of the site. A three-year, $3.5-million adaptive restoration transformed the auditorium into an interpretive center. At left, visitors view a large panel inside the center inscribed with the names of Manzanar's 11,000 internees. Below, the grand-opening celebration for the interpretive center on April 24, 2004, brought more than 2,500 people to Manzanar, including elderly former internees and their families. (Above, courtesy John Bandhauer; left courtesy National Park Service, Manzanar National Historic Site.)

National Park Service ranger Richard Potashin talks to visitors at the cemetery. Rangers began leading tours of the site in 1992. They relate personal stories of all of Manzanar's communities and point out features remaining from each. (Courtesy National Park Service, Manzanar National Historic Site.)

National Park Service arborists continue Manzanar's long agricultural tradition by thinning pear trees planted before 1920 during the site's orchard period. Grafting and installation of new irrigation systems have brought many trees back into production. (Courtesy National Park Service, Manzanar National Historic Site.)

Members of the Modernnaires, a young women's social and sports club at Manzanar War Relocation Center, are shown in 2001 at the annual Manzanar High School Reunion in Las Vegas. (Courtesy Mary Nomura.)

Former residents of the Children's Village orphanage at Manzanar gather in an emotional reunion in Southern California in 1992. Lillian Matsumoto (third row from the top, fourth from the right) headed the orphanage with her husband, Harry. (Courtesy Lillian Matsumoto.)

Gathered here with National Park Service personnel at a May 2004 reunion are children of War Relocation Authority employees. Most had lived with their parents in the staff housing area and attended school in Independence. For many, the reunion was their first meeting in over 60 years. At center front is Martha Shoaf, who taught fourth grade in the camp school. (Courtesy Art Williams.)

Descendants of R. J. Bandhauer, the proprietor of the general store at Manzanar from 1919 to 1925, are shown here in 2004 in front of the store's basement remains at Manzanar National Historic Site. (Courtesy John Bandhauer.)

This iconic image taken at Manzanar by Dorothea Lange captures the ironies and tragedies of Manzanar War Relocation Center. (War Relocation Authority photograph by Dorothea Lange, courtesy National Archives, NWDNS-210-G.)

A windstorm blows up dust near Manzanar in this 1944 photograph by Ansel Adams. (Courtesy Library of Congress Prints and Photographs Division, LC-A35-4-M-32.)

BIBLIOGRAPHY

BOOKS

Bahr, Diana Meyers. *The Unquiet Nisei: An Oral History of the Life of Sue Kunitomi Embrey*. New York: Palgrave Macmillan, 2007.

Burton, Jeffery F., and Mary M. Farrell, Florence B. Lord, and Richard W. Lord. *Confinement and Ethnicity: An Overview of World War II Japanese Relocation Sites*. Washington, D.C.: Western Archeological and Conservation Center, National Park Service, U.S. Department of the Interior, Publications in Anthropology 74, 1999.

Chalfant, W. A. *The Story of Inyo*. rev. ed. Bishop, CA: Chalfant Press, 1933.

Daniels, Roger, Sandra C. Taylor, and Harry H. L. Kitano. *Japanese Americans: From Relocation to Redress*. Seattle: University of Washington Press, 1991.

Garrett, Jessie A., and Ronald C. Larsen, eds. *Camp and Community: Manzanar and the Owens Valley*. Fullerton, CA: California State University, Japanese American Oral History Project, 2004.

Hoffman, Abraham. *Vision or Villainy: Origins of the Owens Valley–Los Angeles Water Controversy*. College Station, TX: Texas A&M University Press, 1981.

Houston, Jeanne Watasuki, and James D. Houston. *Farewell to Manzanar: A True Story of Japanese American Experience During and After the World War II Internment*. Boston: Houghton Mifflin, 1973.

Inada, Lawson Fusao, ed. *Only What We Could Carry: The Japanese American Internment Experience*. Berkeley, CA: Heyday Books, 2000.

Putnam, Jeff, and Genny Smith. *Deepest Valley: Guide to Owens Valley, Its Roadsides and Mountain Trails*. Mammoth Lakes, CA: Genny Smith Books, 1995.

Robinson, Gerald H. *Elusive Truth: Four Photographers at Manzanar*. Nevada City, CA: Carl Mautz Publishing, 2002, 2007.

Walton, John. *Western Times and Water Wars: State, Culture, and Rebellion in California*. Berkeley, CA: University of California Press, 1992.

Wehrey, Jane. *Voices From This Long Brown Land: Oral Recollections of Owens Valley Lives and Manzanar Pasts*. New York: Palgrave Macmillan, 2006.

VIDEOS AND WEB SITES

Remembering Manzanar, A Documentary. Produced by Signature Communications for the National Park Service, 2004.

www.nps.gov/manz

Visit us at
arcadiapublishing.com
·······································